Social Work with Children and Families

Second Edition

EDITED BY
MAUREEN O'LOUGHLIN
AND STEVE O'LOUGHLIN

Series Editors: Jonathan Parker and Greta Bradley

LearningMatters

First published in 2005 by Learning Matters Ltd.
Reprinted in 2006, 2007.
Second edition 2008.
Reprinted in 2008.

British Library Cataloguing in Publication Data
A CIP record for this book is available from the British Library.

ISBN: 978 1 84445 144 9

Cover and text design by Code 5 Design Associates Ltd
Project management by Deer Park Productions, Tavistock
Typeset by Pantek Arts Ltd, Maidstone, Kent
Printed and bound in Great Britain by Bell & Bain Ltd, Glasgow

Learning Matters Ltd
33 Southernhay East
Exeter EX1 1NX
Tel: 01392 215560
info@learningmatters.co.uk
www.learningmatters.co.uk

Contents

This book is dedicated to all the children, young people and families and students we have worked with and who have taught us so much.

Contributors

Julie Bywater is a Senior Lecturer on the Social Work Programmes at the University of Chester. She is an experienced practitioner with both older adults and children and families. She has a particular interest in the involvement of service users and carers in social work education and in the areas of sexuality and social work practice. She is co-author, with Rhiannon Jones, of *Sexuality and Social Work* (2007).

Jackie Hughes is a Lecturer in Social Work at Huddersfield University. She has been involved in social work education since 1983, including at Leeds University, and she is a qualified social worker who has worked with service users and carers in a variety of settings. Jackie is also the parent of a young woman with complex disabilities and her experiences of advocating for her daughter inform both her practice and her teaching.

Maureen O'Loughlin is an independent social work consultant. She was formerly the Director of Social Work programmes at the University of Leeds. She has substantial experience of working with children and families as a social worker, a Guardian ad Litem and in adoption. She undertakes assessments for court proceedings involving children and families and chairs a local authority adoption panel.

Steve O'Loughlin has a particular interest in practice teaching and developed the practice curriculum for the social work degree at the University of Leeds. He is a freelance practice educator and an experienced fostering and adoption worker who undertakes assessments as an independent practitioner. Steve has a particular interest in issues concerning Black children and their families.

Nicky Ryden is a part-time tutor on the Social Work Course at the University of Leeds. She is a social worker with more than 20 years' experience working with Children and Families. Nicky is currently researching for a PhD in the area of young children and social policy.

Introduction

Social work practice with children and families is one of the most challenging, skilled and rewarding areas of social work practice. Social workers work with a diverse group of children and their families, from babies to teenagers, single parents to two-parent families to multi-carer families. Social workers also work with a diverse group of professionals, such as the police, schools, hospitals, health centres and various community organisations. We believe that safeguarding children and preventing them from suffering significant harm is a rewarding and challenging way to make a difference to the life of a child which involves the co-operation, consultation and collaboration of many people working effectively together. This book is itself a collaboration between experienced social work practitioners and educators.

Social workers engaged in this work must believe that the work they do makes a difference and that they can make a difference. In order to do so they must have the necessary knowledge, skills and values to achieve this objective. The introduction of the three-year social work degree has brought changes to the knowledge, values and skills of student social workers. They now need to have knowledge of:

- the national occupational standards key roles;
- the General Social Care Council's (GSCC's) Codes of Practice;
- the law and legislation in relation to children;
- the social and political context;
- a number of different assessment processes in the context of working with children and families;
- interdisciplinary working in an ethnically diverse society;
- different types of family support and substitute care for children;
- working with disabled children.

This book relies on this knowledge to inform the protection of children.

Working with children and families requires many skills: communication, preparation and planning, intervention skills, recognition, identification and assessment of significant harm, recording and report writing, managing oneself and the work, problem solving, research and analysis and decision making skills. This book attempts to review how these skills can enhance working with children and families.

Working with children and families requires that social workers work in a non-judgmental anti-oppressive way. The GSCC's Codes of Practice provide guidance to assist workers in this context. The book explores how social workers' values and attitudes can affect the work they do and the safety of children.

Social work practice with children and families is changing as a result of the many public cases of child abuse. These changes will affect the way services for children are managed, as the role of social service departments changes with the introduction of children's trusts and the more extensive involvement of education departments. Social workers engaged in safeguarding work must be able to work within and between various systems and also manage the work they do effectively. In addition, the registration of social workers with the General Social Care Council has made social workers more personally accountable and responsible for their actions, decisions and conduct. The importance of having a good grounding in working with children and families becomes even more important than ever.

This book is intended to be used by social work degree students and social work educators as well as professional practitioners.

Chapter 1 explores the values and ethics of working with children and families. This chapter will address the social work bench marks 3.1.1 and 3.1.3 which require social workers to have an understanding of social work processes in a diverse society as well as the ethical issues and value dilemmas which face those working with children and families. It will make explicit links to the GSCC Codes of Practice. The chapter seeks to address how values and ethics apply in social work practice with children and families. This chapter will examine issues which arise in working with children and families, and the student will be encouraged to examine their own beliefs and prejudices and the implications for practice that these provoke.

The chapter will discuss the impact of social differences that affect the position of families in society, for example poverty, race, culture, disability and gender. The tensions between welfare principles, children's rights and protection and the right to family life will be considered. Social work practice with children and families will be discussed with reference to interpersonal, institutional and structural discrimination, empowerment and anti-discriminatory practice.

Chapter 2 sets out and explores the changing contexts of social work with children and families over time. It considers the historical context of the work which has informed modern practice. Significant legislation and events are reviewed to try to develop the reader's understanding of how current provision developed. Social work practice is defined in relation to working with children and families and the practical aspects of working with children are highlighted throughout the text. The changes and developments post Climbié are highlighted with brief discussion of Every Child Matters (Department for Education and Skills 2004), the Children Act 2004 and Care Matters (2007).

Chapter 3 focuses on family support, considering current policy and its implications for social work practice. It explores how the provision made to support families in the care of their children varies with the age and circumstances of the child and their family. The impact of poverty will be discussed in the context of supporting families. The aims of family support are also explored and a brief outline is given of the relevant legal knowledge. In addition, the role of the social worker is discussed as an assessor, provider and broker of services. The range of different types of support given to families is also discussed, as is the principle of partnership and the impact 'joined up' thinking can have on the quality of service provided.

Finally, some research findings are reviewed and case studies are presented to illustrate some of the knowledge skills and values that are needed to work with children and their families.

Chapter 4 aims to introduce the student to working effectively with children and families in the safeguarding children arena. It will expand upon the legislative issues raised in Chapter 2 as well as giving definitions of abuse. Safeguarding children will be discussed in the context of the experience of modern families; this will include the impact of domestic abuse, substance misuse and mental ill health. The main elements of the framework of assessment for children in need and their families will be highlighted in the context of multi-agency working. The chapter will discuss the role of the Local Safeguarding Children Boards.

Social work skills and methods of intervention will be discussed and demonstrated at each stage of the safeguarding process with the use of activities.

Chapter 5 covers working with children with disabilities. It will look specifically at the skills required by social workers to support disabled children and their families effectively. It will be based on a social model of disability and promote the values of inclusion for children with disabilities. It will enable students to see disabled children as children first, and build on their skills in communicating with children and undertaking family assessments. It will make links to legislation in terms of the 1989 Children Act Section 17, for children with disabilities as 'children in need' (The Children Act 1989 Guidance and Regulations Volume 6 Children with Disabilities) and the Children Act 2004. It will also refer to the National Service Framework Standard 8 for disabled children and young people and those with complex health needs.

This chapter will look sequentially at some of the issues facing disabled children and their families, building on students' knowledge of human growth and development. Diagnosis, communication, short-breaks and leisure opportunities, education, child protection, housing needs and adolescent transitions will be explored with the use of case studies to enable students to develop skills in working in partnership with disabled children and their families.

Chapter 6 considers the substitute care of children. This chapter will discuss children in the looked after system, reviewing the three main areas of substitute care as well as the Looked After Children (LAC) provisions. Principles of adoption and fostering will be considered in the current legal and social policy context. The processes of adoption and fostering will be outlined using case study material. The chapter will also discuss residential provision as the other area of substitute care, again using case material to highlight principles, procedures and processes.

Throughout the book activities will be used to help you reflect on your values, beliefs and practice. Some of these will focus on the Cole/Green family whose experiences will introduce you to and inform you about social work with children and families.

Chapter 1

Values and Ethics in Social Work with Children and Families

Steve O' Loughlin

Introduction

This chapter will discuss issues which arise in working with children and families in a diverse society. Students will be encouraged to examine their own values and beliefs and the implications these have for practice. The chapter will consider the value requirements for social work practice contained within the GSCC Code of Practice and reinforced by the National Occupational Standards. Anti-oppressive and anti-discriminatory approaches to working with children and families will be discussed and areas of potential conflict highlighted.

The chapter will discuss the impact of social differences that affect the position of families in society, for example poverty, class, race, religion, culture, sexuality and gender. The tensions between welfare principles, children's rights and protection and the right to family life will be considered.

Diversity of families

Social work with children and families rarely involves working with one individual. It will involve working with families that are complex, diverse and constantly changing. The family may consist of one or more parents or carers. It may consist of relative carers such as grandparents, who may be paternal, maternal, or by marriage. The family may consist of non-relative carers such as friends. Additionally, it may consist of parents or carers who share the same race, class, culture, religion and sexuality or alternatively it may consist of parents or carers who have different race, class, culture, religion and sexuality. There may be one or more children in the family, some of whom may share the race, religion and sexuality of their parents and some that do not. To add to the complexity people constantly enter and leave families, by marriage, divorce and death. Millam (2002, p31) describes some of this complexity and diversity when she says that:

> Parents are generally the most important and influential people in a child's life and they usually have more information about their child than anyone else. Some children live with both birth parents, some with one parent, some children live with foster carers, some live in residential homes, and a number of children are adopted.

The child and family social worker will need to both understand and value the complex, diverse and different family forms and be able to assess the relative merits of each one they encounter. The child and family social worker also needs to have a clear idea about why she or he is doing what they are doing as well as being aware of some of the complicated ethical dilemmas which they will encounter. Who is the main focus of the work or intervention, the child or the family? Clearly the child's welfare is paramount, but in order to achieve an outcome for the child work will also need to be done with the family. Before you begin to think about whom you are working with you will need to have an understanding about what you believe is important. The value or importance that you place on the work you are doing and the ethical or moral stance you take, that is simply whether you feel that the work you are doing is right and proper, are the two areas that we are going to explore. As Beckett and Maynard (2005, p1) have stated:

> Values and ethics do not simply exist at the fringes of social work, but are at the heart of social work practice.

I would go further and state that values and ethics are not only at the heart of social work practice but they constitute the life force that permeates every part of social work practice. Having an understanding of what factors might influence your decisions will help to guide your practice. These factors will include personal values and ethics, professional values and ethics, agency values and ethics and societal values and ethics. In order to do this you will need to have an understanding of your personal values and ethics.

Developing an understanding of your own starting point

Think about your personal views and assumptions about how children should be cared for while they are growing up. Make a list of those you feel are most important. How do you think you came to choose these?

Comment

Your list will be personal to you and many factors will influence your views, for example the experiences you have had as a child or parent, as well as your family's or carers' attitudes, beliefs, religion and cultural backgrounds. This list will almost become an internalised standard by which you judge and will be judged by others, except that you also have to consider that your standards might be challenged as being too high, too low, too narrow or too accepting. They are, after all, exclusive to you. Your standards might even be considered to be appropriate for a certain era, and inappropriate or even wrong for the present. A situation which you might like to consider is should you let young children cry or should they be comforted? Your personal views might be that it is okay to let children cry for a while but your professional view will be it depends on how long the child is crying for and whether it is a cry of pain, hunger, discomfort or a cry for attention. Your personal values and beliefs could well mean that you are personally discriminating. It is therefore essential that you also use, understand and adopt some other external standard to guide you. You can do this by considering your professional code of practice. This code or standard list will usually contain things that you should and must do if you are to become a more effective, empowering and thoughtful practitioner.

Professional values and ethics

As a professional you will be committed to certain standards of behaviour and conduct towards service users or the children and their families you are working with. These are outlined in the General Social Care Council (2002) Codes of Practice for Social Care Workers. The Codes of Practice for Social Care Workers are described as:

A list of statements that describe the standards of professional conduct and practice required of social care workers as they go about their daily work.

(GSCC, 2002, p2)

Although the Codes of Practice are not described as values or ethics they do form the basis of the professional values and ethics for social care workers. To put it more simply they should form your professional beliefs about what is important and what is right.

The six main points of the Codes of Practice listed below are divided into sub-sections of between four and eight sub-points. The six main points all begin with the statement: As a social care worker you must:

1. Protect the rights and promote the interests of service users and carers.

2. Strive to establish and maintain the trust and confidence of service users and carers.

3. Promote the independence of service users while protecting them as far as possible from danger or harm.

4. Respect the rights of service users seeking to ensure that their behaviour does not harm themselves or other people.

5. Uphold public trust and confidence in social care services.

6. Be accountable for the quality of your work and take responsibility for maintaining and improving your knowledge and skills.

(GSCC, 2002, p4)

As a children and families social worker you will be protecting the rights and promoting the interests of children and their families. You will be striving to establish and maintain the trust and confidence of children and their families. You will be promoting the independence of children and their families while protecting them as far as possible from danger or harm, always being aware that the child's interests come first. You will also be respecting their rights whilst seeking to ensure that their behaviour does not harm themselves or other people. You will also be upholding the public trust and confidence in you and your employer as well as being accountable for your work and taking responsibility for improving your knowledge and skills.

This Code of Practice contains both professional value statements and professional ethical statements, that is, it seeks to outline what social workers should and must do, as well as how they should be and how they should act (Code of Practice for Social Care Workers 1, 2, 3, 4 and 6).

In number 5 it also sets out what they must not do. It makes clear that workers should be accountable for their work and that they should take some responsibility for maintaining and improving their knowledge and skills as well as acting in a professional manner.

ACTIVITY 1.2

Consider the following situation: you have been asked to go to the house of a family following a referral from a family member who wishes to remain anonymous. The family member states that three children aged 12 years, 3 years and 1 year old are living in unsatisfactory conditions. List some of the things that you might do to meet the Codes of Practice.

Comment

In order to maintain the trust and confidence of the family (Key Role 2) you would need to clearly identify yourself by showing your identity card. You would also respect the family (Key Role 2) by confirming that you have the right family. You would be as honest as you can by explaining the purpose of your visit (Key Role 2) and would protect the rights of children (that includes their welfare and well being) whilst respecting the confidentiality of the source of the referral. You would respect the family (Key Role 2) by asking if you could enter their house to discuss the situation. This would also give the family some degree of choice. If they refused you might need to use your authority and explain your legal duty under the Children Act 1989. By acting in a consistent way with all families you would be meeting (Key Role 5) and attempting to uphold the public trust in children and family social workers. You would do this by not being abusive or confrontational but by being polite but firm.

You are invited to enter the house and are greeted with a living room that looks tidy, clean and well decorated. What goes through your mind – was the referrer malicious, do you leave and apologise for wasting the family's time or do you invade their privacy and dignity further by asking to see the children's bedroom? You reach the top of the stairs and are greeted by the smell of urine. You enter the children's bedroom which has excrement on the floor, holes in the floorboards and in the walls. There are dirty clothes everywhere you look. What decision do you make? Who would you consult with?

As a social worker concerned with protecting children from harm and promoting their welfare you will not only be making individual professional decisions that will be influenced by a code of conduct but you will also need to follow your agency's policies and procedures. These written policies and procedures, together with the unwritten rules of your agency, will together form your agency's values and ethics to which we shall now turn.

Agency's values and ethics

As a professional you will be expected to both act on your own and work as part of a team and consult with others. Your will consult with senior colleagues within your agency about the right course of action. Some agencies will have clearly written guidelines about what you should do and others will leave some things to your discretion.

ACTIVITY **1.3**

Can you think of some of the ways your agency might value and support your intervention in the life of this family?

Comment

How about having a policy that you went out to referrals with another colleague? How about giving you a mobile phone so that you could consult with your colleagues at base and seek some advice if necessary? How about having a culture within your team which is flexible and supportive rather than individualistic?

The first thing you would have to decide is whether the children are at risk of significant harm or are likely to be at risk of significant harm. You may have already come to an initial decision that the children may be at risk if the situation continues and may want to seek your agency's view about precisely what should be done about the situation. The consultations with your agency colleagues might be to suggest that steps should be taken to improve the living conditions of the children immediately. In making this decision you will have to monitor the situation to see if there is any improvement and if not decide whether further action should be taken as well as consider many dilemmas. What are the family's reasons for the current situation? Are there financial issues, class issues (this is how we care for children in our family)? Are there mental ill health issues, is a parent or carer immobilised by illness? Do any of the parents have some kind of disability? Are there issues of how to appropriately control and discipline the children?

ACTIVITY **1.4**

Consider your own beliefs/values about how children should be controlled and disciplined. List what you think are appropriate methods.

Comment

Social workers need to have an awareness of their own beliefs and how these may impact on their work with service users whilst promoting core values of respect and empowerment. However, as you are aware your overriding duty is the welfare of the child you may well be challenging people about behaviours that at one time you accepted without questioning.

Clark (2000) suggests that the core values in social work are concerned with conflict and dilemmas that arise from the dual role of care and control. He identifies eight rules for good social work practice. As well as being personal values these might be some of the core values that your agency might expect of you. They are:

- respectfulness;

- honesty and truthfulness;

- being knowledgeable and skilful;

- being careful and diligent;

- being effective and helpful;

and ensuring that work is:

- legitimate and authorised;

- collaborative and accountable;

- reputable and creditable.

(Clark, 2000, p49)

Have you taken these into consideration in your intervention with the family? Do your agency colleagues share your evaluation of what is dirty and unacceptable? Some may not share your views, some will have rigid and inflexible beliefs and attitudes, which may be based on religious, political or ideological opinions. Collectively, the rigidity and inflexibility of your agency's beliefs and attitudes when transformed into certain behavioural practices may well result in institutional discrimination. You will need to think about how your agency operates as an institution. Do the attitudes and values of certain members of the agency unwittingly discriminate against certain people? Finally, is there anything that this family could not do due to the differences and socially constructed disadvantages that exist in society? It is to the societal values and ethics that we will now turn.

Societal values and ethics

Society places a great deal of importance or value on the care, welfare and well being of children as can be seen in the government's *Every Child Matters* (DfES, 2004) agenda. Families are generally supported providing they are considered to be deserving and conform to society's norms. This is evident from the benefits that are available to a family. For example, Child Benefit is available to all irrespective of wealth or status but a significant number of children live below the poverty line and that number has increased over recent years. But society is changing and evolving; some things, 'which were acceptable in the past' are no longer acceptable today. Beckett and Maynard (2005, p18) describe one of the changes that have occurred in how children are supervised. They state:

> Forty years ago it was normal for children to be allowed to spend long periods away from their homes without parental supervision, playing with friends. Perhaps due to increasing media coverage of incidents where children have been killed or abducted, children are far more restricted now. Parental behaviour that once was regarded as normal, and even healthy, would now be regarded as neglectful and irresponsible.

This illustrates how society's values have changed from being quite liberal to being restrictive or even repressive. It illustrates how what was considered to be an acceptable way of caring for children has been modified by current circumstances and the climate of fear that we live in today, thus becoming a questionable way to ensure children's safety.

Beckett and Maynard (2005, p18) also describe some changes in sexual behaviour. They state:

> In Britain, there has been a huge shift in the last fifty years in what is regarded as acceptable sexual behaviour. Premarital sex is accepted as the norm. Homosexuality has shifted from being a criminal offence to something which MPs and cabinet ministers openly declare. This shift has not occurred in all societies, however.

This also illustrates how society's attitudes and values have changed. As a child and family social worker consider the following activity.

ACTIVITY 1.5

Jane is 14. She confides in you that she is having a sexual relationship with Luke who is 18. You are both Jane's and Luke's social worker, what do you do?

Comment

From the minimal details given above there are several points you would need to think about: first there is your working relationship with Jane and Luke; secondly there is your knowledge that a criminal offence is being committed; thirdly there are the consequences for both parties of any action you might take. Consider what influences you in coming to a decision about what action to take. What factors might make a difference to you, for example if Jane were 10? If Luke were 28? If Jane or Luke had a learning disability or they both had?

The children and family social worker also needs to be able to take account of the different structural perspectives or social differences that influence society's values and ethics if they are to avoid making errors of judgment. The perspectives of age, disability and sexuality have been explored above, but others such as those of black, white, gender, class and religion also need to be considered. Thinking about how these perspectives impact on your practice and your life is probably the hardest thing that you will have to do both as a professional worker and as a person. It will mean that you will have to first accept that you are part of a society which has created the problem in the first place, and its collective attitudes and beliefs can influence you. Is one stronger or more powerful than another for you or do they all exert an equally powerful influence? Can you imagine how they might all be an issue for you? In addition, have you realised that you can become both the oppressor and the oppressed? You will need to accept that your learning in this area will always need to be revised and updated.

In Activity 1.2 you went to see a family with three children. No information was given about the parents. What assumptions or pre-judgments did you make about the parents? Were they both white/UK, was one of them black/UK? Were they two male parents/carers or were they two female parent/carers? How old did you think they were? Create a picture of the parents in your head and imagine going to see them. Now imagine that the female parent is African Caribbean, her name is Donna Green. Her partner is Ahmed Khan and he is the father of the two youngest children, Tariq aged 3 and Nadia Khan aged 1. The eldest child, Kylie Cole aged 12, is African–Caribbean/white and has learning disabilities. Kylie is from Donna Green's previous relationship with Alan Cole who is aged 28. Kylie has contact with her father.

In order to make a fair assessment of the above family there are many factors that you will have to think and learn more about. By being aware of the different perspectives or structural differences that exist you will be more aware of the structural oppression which can be inflicted on children and families and you will have started to adopt an anti-oppressive and anti-discriminatory empowering approach to social work with children and their families. An empowering approach is one that is aware of factors which can negatively impact on families. An empowering approach is one that seeks to promote and enable choice and user self-determination.

ACTIVITY **1.6**

Look at the Code of Practice for Social Care Employees, 2002. Can you identify links between Clark's eight rules (see page 9) and the Code?

Comment

There are clear links between the two, which reflect anti-oppressive and anti-discriminatory practice. Respect is a factor in both, so is honesty, and as is being accountable for the quality of your work and taking responsibility for maintaining and improving your knowledge and skills, Key Role 6.

For the children and family social worker there are no easy solutions. You will have to juggle your personal, professional, agency and societal values and ethics when working with children and their families. Although I have attempted to separate them I think that they are inextricably linked. There will be many conflicts and dilemmas. Throughout the rest of this book you will encounter the Cole/Green family who will present you with further dilemmas. If you think about how the different perspectives might influence the work you are doing with the family you will have begun the process of becoming a reflective, anti-oppressive and empowering practitioner.

In Chapter 2 you will be introduced to a historical account of the legal basis of social work with children and families. When you are reading this account you will need to think about the value of the legislation and how it has changed the way people now work with children and their families. You will also need to think about how difficult it is to change a person's value base or the way a person views the world of children and families. Consider what as a child and family social worker you can do to make a difference to the lives of children who suffer abuse. Can strong values and an ethical empowering approach make a difference? This is something that only you can decide.

In Chapter 3 you will encounter the concept of family support. Supporting families makes good economic sense as they will be able to contribute to the economy rather than exist on state benefits; however this does not take into account either the cost of child care or people preferring to care for their children themselves. This can pose a dilemma for children and family social workers who may become aware that some families who are experiencing poverty are also committing benefit fraud. Which values are the most important: personal, professional, agency or societal? What is the ethical or right thing to do in this situation? There are no easy answers to this dilemma. Personally you might have some sympathy with the family. Professionally and as a member of an agency which has responsibilities of care and control you have a duty to warn the family that they are committing an offence. Also as a citizen of society you have a duty and responsibility to other citizens, as you do to yourself as you are also a citizen.

In Chapter 4 you will encounter issues of child protection. Think about how society's values and ethics have changed towards the care and control of children. Corporal punishment was acceptable in schools, but is no longer. However parents can reasonably chastise their child – it is still lawful to slap a child. It may be acceptable to the parent but is it acceptable to the child? This is a dilemma for children and family social workers, as physical punishment of children has not yet been made illegal.

In Chapter 5 you will encounter the issues around children with disabilities. Think about how society has changed its attitudes towards children/people with disabilities. The provision for children is more inclusive and mainstream than it was in the past, but is it meeting the needs and responding to the wishes of children with disabilities and their carers? The value or importance that society places on children with disabilities has begun to change, community care has replaced institutional care and marginalisation has begun to be replaced by inclusivity and openness.

In Chapter 6 you will be presented with the dilemma of which type of provision is best for children who cannot live with their parents or carers: foster care, residential or institutional care, or adoption. You will also be presented with the dilemma of who can attend reviews. When considering some of these dilemmas you will need to think about how the structure of society, particularly the way society is divided, can lead to oppressive and discriminatory treatment.

This chapter began with an account of the diversity of families and it is appropriate that it should end by asking you to be aware of the influence that ethnicity/race, class, gender, disability, age, religion and sexual orientation may exert on the work you do with children and families. We have looked at some simple definitions of values and ethics and have considered how personal, professional, agency and societal values and ethics may also influence practice.

We also hope that you will continue learning from the high profile child abuse cases that have occurred in the past, such as Colwell, DHSS, 1974; Beckford, 1985; Climbié, DHHO, 2003 where social workers have been criticised for their lack of action and the Cleveland Inquiry (DHSS, 1988). This was appointed because of a perceived overreaction. We hope that you will consider these issues not only whilst reading the book, but during your professional social work career.

FURTHER READING

Beckett, C and Maynard, A (2005) *Values and ethics in social work: An introduction.* London: Sage.
A very readable introduction to values and ethics in social work with many thoughtful exercises to enable the reader to reflect on practice.

Milliam, R (2002) *Anti-discriminatory practice*, 2nd edition. London: Continuum.
Provides the reader with much valuable information as well many practical exercises about anti-discriminatory work with children.

Parrot, L (2007) *Values and ethics in social work practice.* Exeter: Learning Matters.
An easy to understand and thoughtful exploration of values and ethics in social work practice which will further your understanding.

Chapter 2

The Legal and Political Context of Social Work with Children and Families

Maureen O' Loughlin and Julie Bywater

ACHIEVING A SOCIAL WORK DEGREE

This chapter will focus on the legal and political context of social work practice with children and families. It will help you begin to meet the following National Occupational Standards:

Key Role 1: Prepare for and work with individuals, families, carers, groups, and communities to assess their needs and circumstances.

- Prepare for social work contact and involvement.
- Assess needs and options to recommend a course of action.

Key Role 2: Plan, carry out, review and evaluate social work practice with individuals, families, carers, communities and other professionals.

- Interact with individuals, families, carers, groups and communities to achieve change and development and to improve life opportunities.
- Identify the need for a legal and procedural intervention.

Key Role 6: Demonstrate professional competence in social work practice.

- Review and update your own knowledge of legal, policy and procedural frameworks.

It will also introduce you to the following academic standards set out in the social work subject benchmark statement:

2.2.2 Defining principles.

There are competing views in society at large of the nature of social work and its place and purpose. Social work practice and education inevitably reflect these differing perspectives on the role of social work in relation to social justice, social care and social order.

3.1.1 Social work service and service users.

- The social processes (associated with, for example, poverty, unemployment, poor health, disablement, lack of education and other sources of disadvantage) that lead to marginalisation, isolation and exclusion and their impact on the demand for social work services.

3.2.2 Problem solving skills.

- Gathering information.
- Analysis and synthesis.
- Intervention and evaluation.

Introduction

In this chapter we will review the historical context of social work with children and families as well as considering current policy and legislation. The chapter will give an outline of the Children Act 1989 before going on to consider subsequent policy developments and further legislation, which underpin this area of work. The chapter should enable you to have an understanding of the legal and policy context of social work with children and families and some of the implications for practice.

Children and young people have been seen by society in different ways throughout history. It is only comparatively recently that they have been acknowledged as people in their own right whose views should be sought and listened to, as shown in the Children Act 1989 sections 3(a), 22(4)(a), 22(5)(a) for example. Frost and Stein (1989) suggest that children have always had diverse experiences of childhood across culture and class, which illustrates the capacity for affection and cruelty across generations within different societies. However other historians argue that childhood did not exist until the seventeenth century, but agree that the more remote the period of history being considered, the crueller the treatment children experienced (Badinter, 1981). De Mause (1976) suggests that:

> The history of childhood is a nightmare from which we have only recently begun to awaken. The further back in history one goes, the lower the level of child care, and the more likely children are to be killed, abandoned, beaten, terrorised and sexually abused.
>
> (De Mause, 1976, p1)

ACTIVITY 2.1

What do you think were the main areas of concern in society about children and young people in the nineteenth and twentieth centuries?

Comment

Until around 1870 four categories of children were identified in relation to child care concerns by the state. These categories can be summarised as follows:

1. Children of the street (e.g. beggars, prostitutes, etc.).

2. Young offenders.

3. Children at work.

4. Children looked after by the Poor Law authorities (e.g. orphans, children with disabilities, abandoned children, etc.).

None of these child care issues involved direct intervention in the internal aspects of the family until the 1870s (Corby, 2000). We can see from this list that very little has changed; we are still identifying concerns and targeting resources to the same categories of children in 2008. In order to understand the complexities involved in working with children and families, it is important that we have an understanding of how social work practice with children, young people and their families has evolved and been informed by past events and state interventions.

It is therefore useful to review highlights of the preceding two centuries to consider if attitudes and concerns have changed over time.

The nineteenth century

Two of the first pieces of legislation involving the care and protection of children were introduced early in the nineteenth century. The Health and Morals of Apprentices Act 1802, followed by the Factory Act 1833, both focused on children in the workplace rather than in society generally. Other legislation including the introduction of reform schools and the detention of children separately from adults highlighted young offenders as another area of concern in society. Children who were not cared for by their families, or who were ill-treated or neglected, were cared for by the Poor Law Guardians in institutions alongside adults where they received harsh treatment.

There were concerns being raised by individuals and groups about the welfare of children who were looked after in their own families as well as those children who were forced to live on the streets.

- Ambroise Tardieu (1868) a medical professor in Paris described the deaths of children from burning/battering.

- Athol Johnson (1868) noted that children were frequently attending the Hospital for Sick Children in London, having sustained repeated bone fractures. There followed strong resistance from society to his (and the State's) assertion that parents could, and were, deliberately and frequently injuring and harming their own children. More apparently plausible explanations were offered by others to account for his findings, for example, the devastating childhood disease at the time, rickets.

(Any punishment of the perpetrators of child ill treatment was only carried out by family members and neighbours on a personal basis.)

The Infant Life Protection Act 1872 was introduced to address the problem of baby farming followed by the Registration of Births and Death Act in 1874 so that births and deaths could be recorded.

- The London Society for the Prevention of Cruelty to Children was founded in 1884, changing its name to the National Society for the Prevention of Cruelty to Children (NSPCC) in 1889. The NSPCC began to develop a national network of centres and inspectors who became involved in 'rescuing' children from their homes. It is interesting and perhaps ironic to note that the Royal Society for the Prevention of Cruelty to Animals (RSPCA) came into existence 60 years before the NSPCC though concern for the welfare of animals did raise awareness about the plight of children. Ferguson (1990) depicts an NSPCC inspector in 1898 grappling with the same contradictions and complexities as present day social workers.

- Dr Barnardo's, the Church of England Children's Society and the National Children's Homes (all with a Christian religious basis), among other philanthropic organisations, had begun their work and were 'rescuing' children who had fled from, or been abandoned by, their families.

In 1889 the English Prevention of Cruelty to Children Act was passed, and this created the option to prosecute perpetrators of cruelty to children. Police were empowered within the Act to search for children thought to be at risk, and legalised their removal to a place of safety. 'Fit Orders' (now referred to as Care Orders) were imposed on children whose parents had been convicted of offences against them.

Other legislation ensured that children's welfare was considered in custody disputes and began to introduce education for various groups of children including those with sensory impairments (The Elementary Education Act 1870 and the Elementary Education (Blind and Deaf Children) Act 1893).

There was a further dimension to concerns about children which the reports of Charles Booth (1889) and Seebohm Rowntree (1901) highlighted, that of the impact of poverty.

ACTIVITY **2.2**

Can you think of how poverty might have impacted on children in the nineteenth, and twentieth centuries and currently?

Comment

You have probably identified that although there have been many improvements in the quality of people's lives the impact of poverty remains much the same historically as in the present day. Poverty still impacts on the quality of housing, health and education as well as the opportunities which are available to people.

The 1900s

The concerns the reports into poverty highlighted were substantiated by many recruits being rejected on medical grounds when they tried to enlist for the Boer War. The 1904 report of the Interdepartmental Committee on the Physical Deterioration of the Young provided the stimulus for the Education (Provision of Meals) Act 1906 which gave local authorities the discretion to provide food for children who were undernourished. Further provision was made for school medical inspections along with antenatal and child welfare clinics. The 1908 Children Act was one of the first pieces of legislation which addressed a number of issues relating to children rather than focusing on a particular area of concern. The Act established juvenile courts, abolished imprisonment for under 14s and introduced the registration of foster carers. Following pressure from the NSPCC, the Incest Act 1908 was passed. Interfamilial sexual abuse or incest had to that point received little public attention or recognition. Where it was acknowledged, it was linked to low intelligence and overcrowded sleeping arrangements of the poorer classes; another more popular explanation was attributed to the detrimental effects of alcohol (Gordon, 1989).

You can see from the summary above of the provisions made for children that there has been a move from little intervention by the state in family life to an increasing level of intervention, which continues today.

There were some further developments between the two World Wars with the introduction of the first Adoption Act in 1926 (see Chapter 6) and the Children and Young Persons Act 1933 which gave local authorities child protection duties and the power to remove children in an emergency. After the Second World War, according to Douglas and Philpot (1998, p11), the welfare of children was the motor which drove reform. Evacuation had highlighted the poverty in which children lived and through its process left thousands of children separated from their families. The case of Dennis O'Neill (see Chapter 6) also raised public awareness about the plight of children in foster care. The 1948 Children Act sought to address these issues by the introduction of Children's Departments which appointed Child Care Officers and began the process of replacing large institutions with smaller family group homes. The departments began to expand fostering and adoption as alternatives to residential care. This Act emphasised another shift in policy, acknowledging that children who could not live with their families would be better cared for in smaller residential provision or substitute families, policies which continue today.

After the introduction of this Act another gradual shift in focus occurred. Although there had been some provision through legislation to safeguard children from harm there was still a lack of awareness of the extent of child maltreatment and the need for children to be protected.

In 1946 John Caffey (Johnson, 1990) published a paper which became a landmark in the identification of child abuse. There had been developments in radiology in the 1940s which made it possible to date fractures fairly accurately. As a result of this Caffey described unexplained injuries to children; however there was no suggestion at this stage that this was child abuse (Johnson, 1990). Wooley and Evans (1955) were among the first to suggest that adults were causing these injuries to children. Their work was built on by Henry Kempe, an American paediatrician, in 1961. In the UK these developments began to impact with the Children and Young Persons Act 1963 giving local authorities the duty to undertake preventative work with children and families. This reflected an optimistic view that families and local authorities could work together to ensure that appropriate care and conditions necessary for children to develop were maintained. The Children and Young Persons Act 1969 which followed was more focused on child welfare and safeguarding, but also contained elements of control, with one criterion for care order applications being non-school attendance and another beyond parental control. The Act also enabled courts to make place of safety orders which parents could not challenge for 28 days, sometimes resulting in no parental contact during that time.

In 1971 there was a move from specialist Children's Departments to the creation of a generic social work service – available to all and with wide community support, following the Seebohm report (1968) which made recommendations that social work services should be offered in a holistic way within one department.

In 1973 7-year-old Maria Colwell died from physical abuse and neglect. In the months before her death professionals from social services, the police, health, education, the

NSPCC and housing agencies had all been involved with Maria and her family. In 1974 the inquiry into Maria's death criticised the lack of communication between the various agencies involved with the family. This case was crucial in identifying the issues of major social problems and how agencies were to work together. One of the central themes in the Colwell Inquiry was that failures in interagency communication and co-operation were to blame for 'at risk' children not being identified, and provided with protection (DHSS, 1974). (These themes are still relevant today, and were considered in some detail in the Laming Inquiry (2003), see below for further discussions.) In 1975 the child protection register, known until then as the 'At Risk Register', was established as a national requirement for all local authorities to improve contact in such cases between social workers, the police and the medical profession.

During the 1980s it became socially unacceptable to support physical punishment in schools and residential establishments/institutions (however, in 2005, despite many recent parliamentary debates, the law still permits parents to hit their children). Examples from practice, as in the illustration below, indicate opinions differ on what is appropriate chastisement.

A father explained that he had 'only tapped' his 2-year-old son, and had not realised his own strength which had resulted in the boy being hurled against the wall of their home and sustaining a fracture to his arm.

ACTIVITY **2.3**

What are your views on physical punishment and this case illustration. Do your personal views conflict with your duty to safeguard children? Do you think that not realising your own strength is an acceptable explanation?

Comment

Social workers may well have to challenge parents and carers on the appropriateness of the way they control children. You will need to be clear that your primary duty is to safeguard the welfare of the child. This means thinking about the impact on the child not only of physical controls through hitting, restraining, locking in rooms etc. but also on psychological controls and exposure to inappropriate activities.

During the 1980s there were developments which impacted on social work with children and families. In 1984 Kidscape highlighted the problem of sexual abuse and were the first organisation to develop a helpline and introduce awareness programmes in schools.

In 1985 the report of the Jasmine Beckford Inquiry (London Borough of Brent, 1985) was published. Jasmine died aged 4 years in 1984 in an emaciated condition and having been horrifically beaten over an extended period of time by her stepfather, Morris Beckford. Jasmine and her younger sister had been injured in 1981 by Morris, and were taken into local authority foster care with a Care Order being made in 1981. Morris was prosecuted and given a suspended prison sentence. Both Jasmine and her sister were returned home to the care of their mother and Morris Beckford after a six-month period. Over the following two years social services saw Jasmine only spasmodically and she was seen by her social worker only once during the last ten months of her life. The Inquiry made 68 recommendations and stressed concerns that social workers were too optimistic with regard to the families with whom they worked. The report was unequivocal in its view that social work's essential and primary task was to protect children first and consider the rights of parents second, if necessary employing the force of the law to ensure this. Society had begun to realise that children need to be heard. 1985 saw the establishment of Childline, the first phone-in service specifically for listening to children.

In 1986 Child Abuse – Working Together was published as a consultation document (DHSS, 1986). As intervention by the state became more overt, it aimed to make the different responsibilities within the system clear. During 1986 and 1987 statistics regarding child protection registration showed a huge increase in the numbers of children registered following the Beckford Inquiry Report. The numbers prior to this had been at the same level for the previous nine years. There was also an increase in the number of children removed from their homes and taken into the care of the local authorities as a result of child abuse and neglect.

In 1987 a Mori Poll survey suggested that one in ten children had experienced some form of sexual abuse by the age of 15 years; in half of these cases the abuse had been committed either by a family member, or somebody the child knew and previously trusted (Baker and Duncan, 1985). However in Cleveland in 1987, over a period of six months, 121 children were taken into local authority care and long-stay hospital care on Place of Safety orders which parents and carers could not challenge.

There was a general outcry about this with some suggesting that things had gone too far and that parents' rights were being totally disregarded. A public inquiry was set up in 1988 chaired by Lord Justice Elizabeth Butler-Sloss. The Cleveland Inquiry Report (DHSS, 1988) confirmed that child sexual abuse was a more widespread phenomenon than had previously been thought but it also criticised individuals from every agency and professional background for not working together more co-operatively. Social workers were criticised for their too hasty interventions and removal of children and for failing to keep parents informed. This resulted in a change to the Working Together guidelines (DHSS, 1988) which stated that it was inappropriate for parents to attend case conferences. The amendment to the 1988 guidelines highlighted that parents should be invited to attend and placed greater emphasis on interdisciplinary consultation before intervention in sexual abuse cases. It was also recommended that police and social services jointly investigate as a norm.

During this time the legislation relating to children was being re-evaluated as it was fragmented, with different laws applying in custody and welfare with no transfer being possible between courts. Wardship proceedings were used for the most complex cases with subsequent delay in decision making. The resulting Children Act 1989, implemented in October 1991, was a response to the need for a comprehensive piece of legislation, which brought together in one statute many disparate laws relating to children. It introduced new concepts and balances which previous legislation did not have. The Act was also a response both to a number of enquiries into child deaths, which highlighted the need for agencies to work together to protect children, and the need to work in partnership with families using good practice which the conclusions of the Cleveland Inquiry (1988) highlighted as not happening. Section 44(7) of the Act enabled children of sufficient age and understanding to refuse to undergo medical assessments as some of the children involved in the Cleveland investigations had been examined on four separate occasions.

The Children Act 1989 marked a shift in policy from the previous preoccupation with prevention of the reception of children into local authority care, to a broader concept of family support. The Act brought together public and private law to ensure that the welfare of the child is paramount. It was described as:

> *the most radical legislative reforms to children's services of the (last) century.*
>
> (Lord Mackay, cited in Parton, 1991)

The Children Act 1989 sought to balance the protection of children with supporting families whilst introducing and emphasising the concept of parental responsibility, rather than rights. The Act, unlike previous legislation, did not remove parental responsibility from those parents who had it (mothers by right, married fathers and fathers with parental responsibility orders) even though their children might be subject to court orders. The only way of removal was by adoption. Parental responsibility could be limited to some extent if a child was made the subject of a care order but local authorities were no longer able to terminate contact without a court order.

The Act addressed a wide range of issues concerning children: the provision of services for children in need including those with disabilities; the regulation of children's homes; child minding; day care and private fostering. The Act contains specific references to the need to ascertain and listen to the wishes and feelings of children and young people and to take into account their racial, cultural, linguistic and religious background. Additionally the Act acknowledged that young people leaving the care system needed ongoing support beyond the age of 18.

In 1991 the Department of Health published the *Working Together* (DoH, 1991) guidance to support the Children Act 1989 and stressed the importance of working collaboratively across agencies as specifically outlined in section 27 of the Act. Further developments in policy and procedure have lead to this being re-written, the latest version was published in April 2006, its title (*Working Together to Safeguard Children*) reflects the emphasis on 'safeguarding' rather than 'protection' and is indicative of the greater emphasis on consultation and corporate and multi professional involvement in this area, (Department for Education and Skills, 2006).

The early 1990s saw the majority of social work practice with children and families being dominated by child protection section 47 enquiries. Concerns arose about this focus and the lack of support for families before they reached crisis point. Also the lack of services, choice and outcomes for children with disabilities, for care leavers and for children in the looked after system were highlighted with a number of inquiries into abuse in children's homes (see Chapter 6). Rose (1994) suggested that family support and child protection seemed mutually exclusive. She advocated less emphasis on the incident and more on enquiring and assessing whether family support was needed.

Research review

Child Protection: Messages from Research (DoH, 1995a) provides a summary of the main findings of 20 research studies commissioned by the Department of Health into child protection practice. A number of issues were highlighted, including a lack of emphasis on planning and intervention to meet children's needs and the over-representation of African–Caribbean children on child protection registers, whereas Asian children and children with disabilities were under-represented.

The research indicated the need for departments to refocus resources from the almost exclusive emphasis on child protection towards family support.

> *If policy and practice changes are to follow from this round of research, it should reconsider the balance of services and alter the way in which professionals are perceived by parents accused of abusing or neglecting their offspring.*

> (DoH, 1995a, p55)

This, together with the other concerns highlighted above, informed the government's thinking and resulted in a number of initiatives, regulations and pieces of legislation all with the aim of improving services for children, including those who are Looked After, and their families. Those listed below give an idea of the extent of the provisions which have been made between the Children Act 1989 and the White Paper, *Care Matters: Transforming the Lives of Children and Young People in Care*, June 2007.

- **Children's Service Planning Order 1996**
  A legal requirement for local authorities to identify and assess need and then produce plans for children's services in consultation with those requiring and providing services.

- **Quality Protects 1998 (Children First in Wales)**
  Policy initiatives to ensure the safeguarding and improve the quality of care and outcomes for children in the Looked After systems, through establishing specific objectives and the promotion of partnerships between local authorities and other agencies. Objectives include educational achievement and improvement in health, physical and mental.

- **Surestart**
  A further government initiative targeted on areas of deprivation, bringing together early education, health and family support in a way that is accessible to and involves the community.

- **Human Rights Act 1998**
  Requires public bodies such as local authorities to act in accordance with the Convention on Human Rights and offers a way of challenge if they do not (for further discussion see Johns, 2003).

- **Framework for the Assessment for Children in Need and their Families 2000**
  Guidance for assessment in the 1990s had primarily been through that issued by the Department of Health in 1988 known as the Orange Book (DoH, 1988). Government recognised, because of research findings, practice and experience, that guidance on assessment needed to be developed to focus on the needs of children and their families (Horwath, 2001). The Framework offers detailed guidance which maintains a child focus

through providing a systematic way of recording, understanding and analysing a child's developmental needs, the parent's or carer's response to those needs and the wider family and environmental factors which affect the child's situation (see Chapter 3 for further discussion).

- **Children (Leaving Care) Act 2000**
  This Act focuses on the needs of young people of 16 to 17 years who were looked after by local authorities. It gives local authorities the duty to provide a personal advisor and prepare a pathway plan for them. Support and material assistance can be offered until the age of 21.

- **Race Relations (Amendment) Act 2000**
  This act requires public bodies, including local authorities, to work towards the elimination of unlawful discrimination and promote equality of opportunity and good relations between different racial groups.

- **Carers and Disabled Children Act 2000**
  Gives children with disabilities the opportunity of having services commissioned by their parents through direct payments, with increasing responsibility for this themselves as they become adults.

- **Children's Fund**
  The Children's Fund focuses on 5 to 13 year-olds, building on the work of Surestart. It aims to identify children where there are signs of potential difficulty and to provide support to them and their families through multi-disciplinary teams.

- **Children's National Service Framework**
  This initiative sets out standards for the NHS and social services and is intended to break down professional boundaries and achieve partnership working.

- **Care Matters: Transforming the Lives of Children and Young People in Care (2006)**
  Green Paper highlighted the need for children in the Looked After system to have access to a higher standard of corporate parenting which would enable them to be supported to achieve more in their lives.

- **The Children and Adoption Act 2006** provides the courts with new powers to promote contact and enforce contact orders. These include taking part in activities to promote contact (for example programmes or counselling designed to improve contact or to address violent behaviour). The act gives the courts power to make orders requiring participation in unpaid work if someone fails to comply with a contact order or contact activity condition. The act also strengthens the protection for children who are adopted from abroad.

- **Staying Safe (Department for Children, Schools and Families, 2007)** seeks to build on work which is already ongoing to improve the safety of all children and young people, It will include: play and taking part in positive activities in safe environments; understanding and managing risk to help parents and children and young people themselves understand how to keep safe; promoting safer recruitment practices; addressing 'new' threats to children's safety (for example from the internet or mobile phones) and supporting the work of the Local Safeguarding Children Boards.

These examples of government policies and legislation show the range of provisions which are impacting on children and their families in different ways. Following the inquiry into the death of Victoria Climbié (2003) there have been further initiatives through the Children Act 2004 and *Every Child Matters: Change for Children* (2004) which are introducing new and exciting changes to social work practice with children and their families.

Victoria Climbié, as other children have been in the past, was failed by many of the safeguarding professional agencies involved in working with her and her family. The inquiry into her death and the Joint Chief Inspectors' Report on *Safeguarding Children* (DoH, 2003b) were two of the key governmental drivers for change behind the 2004 Act and the *Every Child Matters* (2004) programmes.

These publications have a number of key messages which are underlined in the Act. They include:

- the safeguarding and promoting the welfare of each child;
- the child being the centre of endeavours;
- and that all agencies and their staff must work together.

The messages are being brought into effect in a number of different ways both through policy development and legislation. The Children's Commissioner ensures that a voice for children and young people will monitor the effectiveness of services to improve the well-being of children and young people across the country.

In relation to child protection social work, the Children Act 2004 placed a duty on local authorities to make arrangements with key agencies to improve the well-being and support of children and young people by widening the power of services to pool budgets. The 2004 Act established statutory Local Safeguarding Children Boards to replace the existing non-statutory Area Child Protection Committees. In addition, from April 2006, children's services authorities have been required by regulations to prepare and publish a Children and Young People's Plan (CYPP), which will set out their strategy for services for children and relevant young people (see Sections 10, 11, 13-16 and 17). Databases holding information on all children are being established, along with an integrated inspection mechanism and measures to ensure accountability. The creation of databases seeks to support professionals working together and sharing information, enabling them to identify difficulties and provide appropriate support (see Section 12 of the 2004 Act).

The Children Act 1989 functions of social services have remained unchanged, but how they are delivered at local level has been revised. The Children Act 2004 requires local authorities to lead on integrated delivery through multi-agency Children's Trusts which include health, education, voluntary and independent partnerships. The **Common Assessment Framework (CAF)** for Children and Young People has begun to be implemented by all local authorities from April 2006 to the end of 2008. The CAF is part of the wider *Every Child Matters: Change for Children* programme. Along with other elements, including the role of the lead professional, multi-agency working and the introduction of information sharing data bases as outlined earlier, it should help agencies to provide a more integrated service to children, young people and families. The CAF aims to help practitioners assess children's additional needs earlier and more effectively (DfES, 2004).

The introduction of the CAF will be an important part of the strategy to shift the focus from dealing with the consequences of difficulties in children's lives, to preventing things from going wrong in the first place (risk minimisation). It should help children and young people, supported by their parents or carers, to achieve the priority outcomes to:

- be healthy;

- stay safe;

- enjoy and achieve;

- make a positive contribution;

- achieve economic well-being.

If a CAF suggests that a child has needs that require input from more than one service, one practitioner will act in the role of lead professional to:

- provide a single point of contact whom children, young people and families can trust, and who is able to support them in making choices and in navigating their way through the system;

- ensure that children and families get appropriate interventions when needed, which are well planned, regularly reviewed and effectively delivered;

- reduce overlap and inconsistency from other practitioners.

(DfES, 2004, pp2–4)

It will not be necessary to do a common assessment for every child; a checklist will be used to decide whether a CAF is needed or not. The CAF has been designed so that with appropriate training practitioners from any discipline will be able to complete it. This is to help address the tensions in cases where several professionals are involved in the completion of assessments within the current Assessment Framework. Currently social workers have predominantly been left to compile the information in the assessment with health visitors, teachers, community psychiatric nurses, etc. providing verbal summaries in core group meetings. The CAF is part of a wider programme to provide more integrated services. It seeks to improve multi-agency working by being an accessible tool using a common language and maintaining a single overview record of the needs and progress of a child in contact with several agencies.

It should hopefully begin to address the problem, highlighted in so many inquiries, of communication between agencies which effectively prevented them working together. It is an opportunity to be seized upon by all those who work with children.

The changes introduced by the Children Act 2004 have been expanded on through the Care Matters agenda to focus particularly on Looked After Children. These include more social work time for children and young people; better support for carers and improved educational opportunities for Looked After Children. It is envisaged that there will be more opportunities for training and apprenticeships, with stronger emphasis on health and support for care leavers for longer. After a period of consultation a White Paper has been produced (July 2007), the Government has stated that it will seek the 'earliest opportunity' to amend the current legislation around children and young people in the Looked After system. Pilot programmes have begun in some areas, for example in intensive treatment for children in foster care, a Family Drug and Alcohol Court and Children's residential care Pedagogy. Developments are planned to pilot independent Social Work Practices (small groups of social workers undertaking work with LAC children commissioned by, but independent of, local authorities) these developments and others will continue during 2008 with statutory guidance and National Minimum Standards being anticipated in 2009.

C H A P T E R   S U M M A R Y

The area of children and family law and policy is complex. This chapter has introduced you to both the historical context and the current provisions. The historical context has shown you how law and policy have developed over time, highlighting the concerns which have been repeated in a number of inquiries as well as showing how the focus of work has changed and is changing. The chapter concludes by briefly considering the Children Act 2004, Every Child Matters, Care Matters and the Children and Adoption Act 2006 and the Staying Safe provisions. These seek to address the underlying problems of multi-agency working which have so impacted on children and their families (whether through child protection issues, children in need or with disabilities or for those being looked after). They acknowledge and reaffirm that corporate responsibilities for children must be more appropriately fulfilled and contact promoted following parental separation if the lives of vulnerable children and young people are to be safeguarded and supported to enable them to achieve their potential.

FURTHER READING

Department of Health and Home Office (2003) *The Victoria Climbié inquiry: Report of an inquiry by Lord Laming.* London: The Stationery Office.
Reading this report will help you gain an understanding of why things go wrong and why partnership working is so important.

Department for Education and Skills (2004) *Every child matters: Change for children in social care.* London: The Stationery Office.
Useful reading to gain a fuller understanding of the new provisions for children post Climbié.

Department for Education and Skills (2006) *Working together to safeguard children.*
Useful reading to gain a fuller understanding of the expectations of all those with responsibilities for safeguarding children.

DCFS (2007), White Paper, Care matters: Transforming the lives of children and young people in care, June. The Stationery Office.
Reading this document will give you some understanding of the Government's plans for significant changes for children in the Looked After system.

WEBSITES

www.dfes.gov.uk provides access documents and continuing developments within the Every Child Matters agenda as well as useful statistical information.

www.doh.gov.uk – likewise provides useful background information and statistics.

Chapter 3

Family Support in Social Work with Children and Families

Nicky Ryden

3.1.4 Social work theory.
- Research-based concepts and critical explanations from social work theory base of social work, including their distinctive epistemological status and application to practice and disciplines that contribute to the knowledge.
- The relevance of psychological and physiological perspectives to understanding individual and social development and functioning.

The subject skills highlighted to demonstrate this knowledge in practice include:

3.1.5 The nature of social work practice.
- The nature and characteristics of skills associated with effective practice, both direct and indirect, with a range of service users and in a variety of settings including group care.

3.2.2 Problem solving skills

5.2.1 Knowledge and understanding.
- Ability to use this knowledge and understanding in work within specific practice settings.

Introduction

This chapter will first define family support and then explain how the concept has developed over time so that you will be able to locate your practice in what can be a complex picture. It will explore the characteristics of family support and the related social work practice, how needs are defined, the importance of the assessment process, the need for planning of any intervention and reviewing of that intervention in ways which are sensitive to the individual circumstances of children and their families. It will provide case examples of family support interventions for different problems and outcomes.

Definitions of family support

In 1994 the Audit Commission produced a report on services for children which used the following definition of family support:

> *Any activity or facility provided either by statutory agencies or by community groups or individuals aimed at providing advice and support to parents to help them bring up their children.*

> (Audit Commission, 1994, p39)

There is an emphasis here on the providers as experts, who can 'advise and support' parents on bringing up their children, rather than a partnership approach, which would see rearing children as the responsibility of all adults in a society, not just of their parents.

A more inclusive definition is one used by Barbara Hearn:

> *Family support is about the creation and enhancement with and for families in need, of locally based (or accessible) activities, facilities and networks, the use of which have outcomes such as alleviated stress, increased self esteem, promoted parental/carer/family competence and behaviour and increased parental/carer capacity to nurture and protect children.*

> (Hearn, 1995, p6)

The emphasis here is on local provision to overcome the stresses that can make parenting a difficult task. You will notice that this definition refers to families in need, which we will explore later when we consider the families services are provided for and the nature of those services.

Comment

You may have noted that 'family' usually consists of adults and children living in the same place; that those people will have a relationship with each other that might be defined in biological, emotional or legal terms, and that there might be dependency and mutual support as well as conflict and violence. You may have considered the different kinds of families of which you have knowledge, one parent families, stepfamilies, adoptive families. You might have considered 'family' in terms of responsibility, arguing that the adults are responsible for the care and upbringing of the children so that they reach their potential and in their turn contribute to the community by working and rearing their own family.

Similarly with support, generally we use this to mean a prop or framework which will keep something upright, often a growing thing. We use it in terms of emotional support, friendship and relationships which promote our sense of belonging to a community. Support can be practical as well as emotional; in fact one could argue that without practical support other forms of support will not be effective.

When we put the two words together, 'family support', we have a term which might lead us to consider the multiplicity of family groups, the way that families change over time, often splitting and reforming with other individuals or parts of other families. Those families will be expecting and seeking support in the task of raising their children from a whole range of informal and formal support networks; friends, relatives, schools, health services, local authorities and government. Clearly we are dealing with complex relationships, not only between family members, but between families and the state.

The development of family support

There is considerable debate on whether services for children and families should be universal or targeted and on the purpose and intention of the state when it promotes such services. Historically in Britain there has been a reluctance to intervene in the privacy of family life, or to tell parents how they should discipline their children. Until the Welfare State was set up after the Second World War, provision for those who could not support themselves and their children was shaped by the Poor Laws. The Poor Law Relief Act, 1601, provided out relief, a small weekly payment which allowed the person or family to remain in their home. The Poor Law Amendment Act, 1832, decreed that the able bodied poor could only receive support if they entered the workhouse. For families this often meant being separated, with little hope of reunification. Generally any provision was designed to discourage people from seeking support. A number of concerned individuals started organisations to support and rescue children who were orphaned or abandoned, to supplement the provision made by the workhouse, for example Dr Barnardo's and The Children's Society. Voluntary organisations continue to have a significant role in providing family support services. Holman (1988) reviews the way that statutory and voluntary agencies developed preventive strategies so that children could be maintained in their own family, rather than in institutions or the homes of strangers.

The role of the social worker in supporting the family

With the launching of the Welfare State in 1948, health and education became universal services for children and their families. The financial support of the family in times of unemployment, of ill health or disability was ensured, the introduction of the Family Allowance gave every family with more than one child a weekly payment to meet the costs of raising children. When it came to considering support and advice for families it was not considered necessary to have universal services. The Children Act 1948, did not consider prevention, but was concerned with setting out the circumstances in which the local authority would take over the responsibility of parenting children and with the ways in which it would undertake that task. However, the new Children's Officers were soon arguing that in many cases earlypractical advice and support could avoid the need to receive children into the care of the local authority. Many families living in areas of social deprivation found the new Children's Department a useful source of advice on dealing with children's behaviour or developmental problems. Caring for children at times of intolerable stress or distress helped many families over difficult periods. In 1963 the Children and Young Person Act gave the local authority the power to give practical and financial support to prevent children coming into care.

Lorraine Fox-Harding has given us a useful way of examining the principles that underlie social work practice with families. Fox-Harding's *Perspectives in Child Care Policy* (1991) outline the relationship between the State and the family. She calls the first perspective laissez-faire and paternalism, which characterises the situation where the family is defended from interference by the State unless the child is harmed by its parents or the child is an offender. On those occasions the State, or its representative the social worker, has a right to intervene, but in the interests of maintaining minimal public expenditure most families will be regarded as of no concern to the State.

The next perspective develops from the recognition that children can be the victims of poor parental care and that they deserve to be rescued from such care – this is called State paternalism and child protection. The goal of any intervention is to remove the child from such harmful care and place them in a substitute family, to give the child a fresh start. The 1976 Adoption Act gave local authorities the opportunity to apply for children to be freed for adoption so that children could be established in new families, over-ruling the objections of their birth parents. In reaction to this power of the State the third perspective, defence of the birth family and parent rights, developed. Fox-Harding calls this the modern defence of the family to distinguish it from the original laissez-faire approach and in this she argues the State is providing support for families so that children do not need substitute care:

This may take the form of intensive help directed to those families on the verge of breaking up, or of broader social policies to support all families with children.

(Fox-Harding, 1991, p71)

The Children Act 1989, with its emphasis on parental responsibility and partnership between parents and social workers in resolving concerns about children, reflects this perspective. The maintenance of family links is central to the Act, when a child has to be cared for by the local authority parents retain their parental responsibility.

Finally, her fourth perspective is that of children's rights and child liberation, in which the child is seen as a subject in their own right, with rights and freedoms similar to those of an adult. This perspective has encouraged adults to listen to and to take account of children's own views about their lives and the services provided for them.

Recent developments in family support

Since 1997 there has been a concerted effort by the government to address the issue of social deprivation and of family stress. This implies a shift in thinking about the position of children in our society, from being the sole responsibility of their parents to one of social investment, that is, the State has an interest in promoting the health and development of all children as a means of ensuring the future stability of society (see Frost, 2003, pp7–9 and Featherstone, 2004 pp96–100).

In 1998 the Home Office produced a document called *Supporting Families: A Consultation Document*, in which the government outlined a new, supportive and preventive approach to families and children. In particular it recognised that living in deprived circumstances operated to make parenting more challenging and caused children to not reach their potential, with implications for the future prosperity of the country. Supporting Families outlined for the first time how the State might actively support parents in parenting, whilst also encouraging as many adults as possible to enter the labour force – to achieve this goal parents need to have reliable and affordable childcare. The high costs to society of family breakdown, particularly if it led to delinquency and offending, was to be overcome by investing in preventive strategies with young families. The following year the Department of Health issued *Opportunity for All: Tackling Poverty and Social Exclusion*, which launched a number of initiatives, increased investment in Early Years education; the launching of Sure Start; the National Child Care Strategy for affordable quality childcare for children aged 0-14 years, and Connexions, an advisory service for young people in education. The report outlined various financial supports to poorer families such as Working Families Tax Credits and Educational Maintenance Allowances.

Since *Supporting Families* was published, large sums of money have been invested in improving the quality of provision for education and health services for all children. The Government has promoted the development of pre-school care for more and younger children. The agencies responsible for providing services are being restructured with children's services being separated from those provided for adults. This new policy was first articulated in *Every Child Matters*, a Green Paper produced by the Treasury in 2003. In the introduction Paul Boateng writes:

We must be ambitious for all children, whoever they are and wherever they live. Creating a society where children are safe and have access to opportunities requires radical reform.

(Treasury, 2003, pp3–4)

The Children Act 2004 has formalised this call for radical reform, identifying five outcomes for children: being healthy, staying safe, enjoying and achieving, making a positive contribution and achieving economic well-being (Her Majesty's Government, 2004, p4). Alongside these universal aspirations for all children is a new framework for safeguarding children, with an emphasis on multi-agency co-operation and working (DoH 2006).

Provision of family support

There are a wide variety of organisations and services that can be considered to provide family support. Some will be befriending schemes, depending on volunteers who have had similar challenges to face, e.g. Homestart, others may have a long history of supporting families living in areas of social deprivation, e.g. Family Service Units. Other projects may come under the umbrella of large voluntary organisations such as Barnardos or the Children's Society; others will be run by statutory organisations. Family support is not limited to families with pre-school children. There are a wide range of projects and services which are provided by both statutory and voluntary agencies across the country. Frost has argued that this represents a progressive form of welfare practice (Frost, 2003) at a time when globalisation and rapid social change are impacting on families, creating diverse family structures and challenging traditional role models of parenting. The significance of having a choice of service providers may be particularly significant for black and ethnic minority families, who find it difficult to access services which do not reflect their culture (Butt and Box, 1998a; 1998b; Butt, 1998), or who may feel their parenting style is not understood by white workers. In the same way expertise in dealing with particular problems, for example drug and alcohol dependent parents, may deliver more effective services for those families than a more generic service (see Frost, et al., 2003).

The provision of family support by child welfare agencies has often been located in Family Centres. Such centres have been around for about forty years; this approach to delivering services invited all of the family to attend, to benefit from advice and support, to access educational opportunities, to give the children play opportunities. Family Centres have been categorised according to their function:

- the client focused model;

- the neighbourhood model;

- the community development model.

(Holman, 1987)

The client focused model offers specialised activities, only accepts referred clients, often draws it users from a wide area and the workers will be professionally trained. Often such centres will be concerned with working with families where there are child protection issues and may also undertake core or specialist assessments of family functioning for court proceedings. This model of Family Centre will often be wholly funded by the Local

Authority, or have an agreement with the Local Authority to work with families who have complex needs.

The neighbourhood model is integrated with its local community, has an open door policy and will encourage local volunteers to contribute to the activities and programmes. Any paid staff are likely to be flexible in the roles they undertake, responding to individual need and day to day demands. This model of Family Centre will often be funded by a local trust or voluntary organisation, and will be well used by local families.

The community development model is similar in many respects but has a philosophy which is focused on developing the community, encouraging local residents in taking control of the local resources and making management decisions. Both neighbourhood and community centres can make a significant difference for children in need by improving play opportunities, developing social activities for families with children and by offering advice and support to stressed parents.

There is another model of family centre, the integrated model, which incorporates all of these aspects; some are nationally known. For example Pen Green in Corby (Koris, 1987; Makins, 1997; Whalley 1994) is based on an old secondary school site and is well known for its creative and varied approach to supporting families by providing specialist programmes as well as education access programmes, day care and out of school resources for children of all ages and a full programme of activities for both men and women. Another such centre is the Fulford Family Centre in Bristol (Stones, 1994). The integrated model of the family centre (Warren, 1998) can be identified in the government thinking about Children's Centres, where the intention is to co-locate all local services for children so that they work effectively together and are accessible to all children.

Family centres continue to provide support to families, although many are now developing new partnerships and roles as the government has launched a series of new initiatives to improve provision for young children and to address the implications of childhood poverty. (See Tunstall, et al., 2006)

RESEARCH SUMMARY

Family Support at the Centre: Family Centres' Services and Networks *is a study which consisted of a postal survey of 400 family centres and interviews with managers of 40 family centres, interviews with over 100 families who used centres and a postal questionnaire of 60 professionals who had links with family centres.*

The study found that family centres acted as gateways to services by:

* *providing services themselves;*

* *joint work with other agencies;*

* *having links, both formal and informal, in the community.*

The centres provided advice and support to parents by direct work with parents on issues of importance to them; by networking and multi-agency work on behalf of the family, ensuring they had access to the services they needed; by co-ordinating services for families in need (often the centre was a primary provider of services); having staff with varied backgrounds and training, who could be flexible and creative in meeting the needs of the family and the demands of funders for particular kinds of services.

The study showed that centres often were subject to pressures to change their style of service delivery in response to the changing priorities of their funders, who were dealing with changes of policy and strategy by central government. Many centres found that decision making moved outside of the centre, with restrictions on who could use the service and what the service should look like. Particularly when the main funder was Social Services there would be pressure to provide 'core' services, such as assessment interventions to reduce risk to children such as parenting programmes, rather than subsidiary services which might have promoted personal and social development of children and their parents. Many centres had to work hard to maintain an open gateway for families. Planning was made more difficult by the way funding is provided, often short term for closely defined purposes, with large projects needing to apply to a number of sources with little guarantee of success.

The study concluded that family centres are well placed to provide community based services for children and families. Most centres had a positive view of parents and sought to use a strengths-based approach in their work with families. However there has been a growing trend towards specialisation, to focusing on families where children are at risk, rather than on families in need.

The authors conclude:

This is especially unfortunate because the strengths centres possess are at the heart of government policy to support families and enhance the developmental welfare of children. Through their holistic approach to families, centres can balance individual family members' needs and wants with the needs of children and young people and take a long term view of service provision.

(Tunstill, et al., 2004, p258)

Sure Start

In the late 1990s the New Labour government established a review of policy for pre-school children, which cut across a number of government departments and was chaired by the Treasury (www.surestart.gov.uk). The process of consultation between government departments and with recognised authorities on early years' provision, visiting sites of Early Excellence, gave rise to the Sure Start Programme. Each programme has its own partnership arrangements for management and governance, including voluntary and statutory agencies, parent representatives, community members, private sector representatives. The programme was launched in 2000, targeted on the poorest communities, and has been consistently expanded year by year.

Sure Start programmes provide support to all families with children under 5 years, in the areas where they are located, by providing a range of resources relevant to families with young children, home visiting to support stressed parents, running parenting programmes and drop-in centres, offering health advice and support, promoting educational opportunities to help adults acquire new skills, ante-natal services, postnatal screening for depression, advice on breastfeeding, home safety advice and equipment loan. Many programmes also provided new childcare places or play and learning opportunities for children (Tunstill, et al., 2002). The National Evaluation of Sure Start (NESS) has so far produced findings which suggest that the centres are having difficulty in reaching the most socially excluded families including those from Black and Ethnic Minority communities. So far there is little evidence that the provision is having much impact on children's attainment, although it is recognised that indicators of children's increased resilience will not be demonstrable until they reach their teens. (www.bbk.ac.uk/ness, Lloyd and Rafferty 2006, National Audit Office 2006)

Children's Centres

Following the publication of *Every Child Matters* (2003) the government announced in December 2004 that it was extending the Sure Start programme by opening Sure Start Children's Centres in every community. These centres would extend the existing Sure Start provision by providing affordable day care. The target is to have 3,500 centres by 2010. Although this appears to be a universal service, it is in fact targeted, with centres in the 30 per cent most deprived communities being required to provide core services which include integrated childcare and early learning, in other words a structured learning environment for young children, whilst in less deprived areas the core service must include 'drop-in activities' for children and families. All Children's Centres are expected to promote parental employment, to offer integrated child and family health services, outreach and family support, support for childminders and for children and parents with special needs.

Extended Schools

Besides services for pre-school children the 2002 Education Act allows school governing bodies to provide, through partnerships with providers, a range of services to support children and families. Based on *Every Child Matters*, the goal for 2010 is for every school to offer high quality wrap around care for children from 8am to 6pm. There are core services of after school activities, including study support, parent support, effective referral to specialist support services and community access to ICT, sports and arts facilities. Children will therefore be spending more hours at the school site, which will become more accessible to the community. The *Aiming High for Children* (DfES 2007) outlines the government's strategies for building resilience amongst families caught in a 'cycle of low achievement'. These interventions are targeted at children who are in receipt of free school meals and include two hours of free activities per week, with two weeks of holiday activities. The new Department for Children, Schools and Families will be driving this agenda forward, encouraging parents to raise their expectations for their children with a Parents' Charter. Professionals are urged to be proactive in engaging with such families, providing integrated services tailored to their needs. To assist schools, health professionals and other children's services it is proposed that the Common Assessment Framework be available electronically. As part of the extended school's agenda the Connexions service which provides an advice guidance and personal development service in English schools for 13-19 year olds is being reorganised.

Children and families in need

The Children Act 1989 introduced the concept of a child in need and outlined the duties and responsibilities of the local authority in respect of such a child. Section 17 states that:

> *It shall be the general duty of every local authority . . .*
> *(a) to safeguard and promote the welfare of children within their area who are in need; and*
> *(b) so far as is consistent with that duty, to promote the upbringing of such children by their families, by providing a range and level of services appropriate to those children's needs.*
>
> (HMSO, 1989, p12)

The Act goes on to say that the local authority can ask voluntary agencies or other individuals to provide such service on its behalf, that assistance can be in kind or in exceptional circumstances cash, that any assistance can be subject to a means test, but if the family is dependent on benefits then they will not be liable to repayment of assistance. It then defines a child in need:

> *. . . a child shall be taken to be in need if:*
> *(a) he is unlikely to achieve or maintain, or to have the opportunity of achieving or maintaining, a reasonable standard of health or development without the provision for him of services by a local authority under this Part;*
> *(b) his health or development is likely to be significantly impaired, or further impaired, without the provision for him of such services; or,*
> *(c) he is disabled,*
> *and family in relation to such a child includes any person who has parental responsibility for the child and any other person with whom he has been living.*
>
> (HMSO, 1989, p13, see also Johns, 2003, pp46–9)

The Act defines disability in terms of sensory deficit, mental disorder and substantial or permanent handicap by illness, injury or congenital deformity, then goes on to define development as meaning physical, intellectual, emotional, social or behavioural development and health as physical or mental health.

As you can see, the definitions given in the legislation seem to have little relationship to any real child and their family. It also suggests that there are universally understood and accepted standards of health and development. Clearly having a disability means a child is in need, but what is a disability? Being without hearing, sight or speech are disabilities according to the Act, but does suffering chronic inner ear infections also qualify a child as in need? If it could be argued that the infections meant time off from school and that when able to attend the child was unable to learn effectively because of hearing loss, then perhaps they would be regarded as in need, but what kind of service might they or their family require? If the child has parents who are responsive to the need for treatment then the child will be attending the audiology clinic and getting the help necessary to minimise the impact of the hearing loss. If the child has parents who are careless about keeping appointments, or who are not concerned about the child missing school, then there might be a case for intervention, because without help this child is not going to achieve a reasonable standard of health or development. The intervention might take the form of encouraging the parents to take the child to see the appropriate professionals, perhaps providing practical support to attend if the family live in an isolated place or have difficulty with transport.

CASE STUDY

Let us consider Kylie, who is 12-years-old, and of mixed parentage, African-Caribbean/White. She lives with her mother Donna and sees her father Alan Cole regularly. Donna was in care as a child, she did not get much education, she says Kylie is like her, not much good at school. Kylie does not like school, where she says she is bullied by other girls, who call her names. Kylie is small for her age, she is not well dressed. Kylie has attended school 60 per cent of the time in the last term.

ACTIVITY **3.2**

Spend some time thinking about Kylie. Do you think she is a child in need? Who is her family? What kind of provision might the family welcome?

Comment

It appears that Kylie is a child who finds school a difficult place to be and whose mother may not place much value on education. In this respect she may be like many other children who attend that school. Living with a single parent who is on benefit will mean that money for clothes is in short supply. The local authority may assist with the provision of school clothing. Would there be any need to do more than ensure that the family is receiving all the benefits to which they are entitled? The local authority has a duty to target its services on those most in need – so within the local area Kylie and her family may not be amongst those families.

The Children Act Report 2002 highlighted the high thresholds Social Services Departments were operating for children in need if there was no evidence of risk of significant harm (DfES, 2002, p33). The Children in Need Census, which collects information on all children referred over seven consecutive days, showed that 15,400 cases were dealt with, within the first 24 hours (DfES, 2002). In many instances the decision will be that no service will/can be offered.

The government funded a series of research studies evaluating the way services for children in need were being implemented (Colton, et al., 1995; Aldgate and Tunstill, 1995, DoH, 1995). Earlier research had suggested that local authorities had misinterpreted the Act and not appreciated that they had as much responsibility for children in need as they had for children who were at risk and in need of protection. Contrary to the Act's intention services for children and families in need had been service led rather than needs led – in other words provision had been determined on the basis of reducing demands for more expensive services such as providing accommodation for children, rather than responding to social deprivation. It had also established that families who did receive family support were generally eager for advice and support, particularly when concerned about adolescent behaviour problems and involvement in offending.

RESEARCH SUMMARY

Services for children in need

This study looked at children referred to seven Social Services departments under Section 17 but excluding children with a disability. In all the study looked at 93 children and their families. Besides other means of collecting data, 41 of the children were interviewed for the study. Needs arose from the particular child or from family circumstances affecting a particular child. There were more boys than girls, the boys were more likely to have needs associated with offending behaviour and girls to have needs associated with social deprivation. If children were under 6 their needs were likely to be related to family stress, parental ill health and social deprivation. Between 7-12 years needs arose from family stress and social deprivation and for those aged 13-16 years from offending behaviour, family stress and deprivation. Families living in social deprivation were more likely to refer themselves and generally problems were either acute, usually needing short-term interventions, or chronic which required longer-term social work support and work alongside other agencies.

The research found that people were hoping for support and advocacy in relation to their problems, for help with child development, improvement in family relationships and alleviation of family problems. Half the families in the study were looking for help with family relationships, 40 per cent of the children were hoping that parental conflicts would be resolved. People wanted social work support, child and family centred services such as respite care or day care and practical help.

Families who referred themselves were less likely to receive a service than those who were referred by another professional, with those families receiving more services over a longer period. The service provision varied with the need, cases of social deprivation were least likely to get a service, whilst family ill health was more likely to receive a service. Often a wider range of services was offered than had been requested, so requests for accommodation might be met with offers of day care, activities or short-term accommodation.

Generally people found Social Services sympathetic and helpful, with most people feeling they had received more benefits than they had expected. Half of the children were pleased that Social Services had been involved and were happy with the services offered (Tunstill and Aldgate, 2000).

The research by Tunstill and Aldgate used the following categorisation of children in need:

- *The child has an intrinsic need, relating to their own physical condition or developmental delay.*

- *The child is in need because of parental illness, mental or physical, addiction, depression or severe stress.*

- *The child is in need because of family stress.*

- *The child is in need because of offending behaviour.*

- *The child is in need because of social deprivation.*

This categorisation of needs is based on that produced by Sinclair and Carr-Hill (1997). It gives us a more meaningful definition for understanding what family support activity is attempting to address.

CASE STUDY

Let us return to Kylie, whose school has referred her to Social Services. Kylie's teacher is concerned about Kylie's non-attendance at school, about the way her mother does not seem able support Kylie in getting to school regularly and about what Kylie has told her about home. There are two younger children who Kylie babysits for, often until quite late at night. The teacher feels that Kylie is not really mature enough to cope with the responsibility. Although Kylie's mother Donna is wary of social work involvement, she does want some help, as her partner is often out visiting friends or working. Having two pre-school children is hard work, and the 3-year-old, Tariq, is very demanding.

Donna says she would like Kylie to have somewhere to go after school and during the holidays because she has her hands full with the little ones. Donna is not sure that she wants any help with Tariq, although she admits his tantrums and demanding behaviour get her down. Donna's partner Ahmed Khan is not there when the social worker visits. Kylie tells her that she likes helping her Mum look after the little ones and that she would like to make some friends.

The social worker knows that a Sure Start programme is starting soon on the estate where the family live. She tells Donna about the playgroup and the opportunity for her to meet other mothers and perhaps attend a keep fit class. There is also an after school club starting at the junior school and although Kylie is 12, she is immature and perhaps she would be happier there than in a group with her own age group. The social worker offers to send Donna the information on Sure Start and to make a call to the after school club organiser to talk about Kylie attending. Donna agrees with this and waits for the information to arrive.

Later Donna receives a visit from the Sure Start co-ordinator who is visiting all local families to tell them about what the new centre is offering and to encourage everyone to attend the open day. The social worker rings Donna to tell her Kylie can go to the after school club, and it will cost £1 per session. The social worker makes a further call after two weeks to ask Donna how things are going. Donna tells her Kylie has been to the club and enjoyed it, and that she is going to take Tariq to the Sure Start playgroup. One month after receiving the initial referral the case is closed.

The assessment process

On receiving a referral the Social Services Department has one working day to decide whether to take any action. The team manager has noted there are two younger children who may be being supervised by someone who may not be a responsible person. There is no suggestion the children are at risk, so the case is classed as 'a child in need'. It is noted that Donna was herself in care as a child and that there was some contact when Kylie was younger. The decision is made to make an initial assessment. This must be completed within seven working days. The initial assessment will determine what action may need to be taken. Enquiries will be made of other agencies, e.g. the health visitor and GP, the school and the family. Because Kylie is 12 the social worker will speak to her on her own to discover what Kylie's wishes and feelings are about having help. The Framework for the Assessment of Children in Need and Their Families was issued by the government in 2000 to ensure that children's needs are fully and consistently assessed, using a holistic approach.

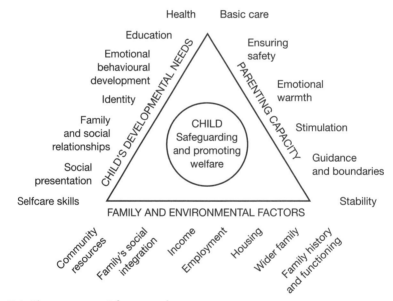

Figure 3.1 *The assessment framework*

Source: Department of Health (2000). *The framework for the assessment of children in need and their families.* The Stationery Office.

The Framework encourages social workers to look at family strengths as well as identifying the difficulties. In Kylie's family there are strengths: Donna has raised Kylie more or less on her own, although her school attendance is not as good as it should be and there is no suggestion that Kylie is involved in any anti-social activity when she is not in school. Kylie has said she is being bullied and that might account for her frequent stomach aches and eagerness to stay home to help her mother. Although Donna is finding Tariq's behaviour challenging the children are otherwise healthy and apparently well cared for. Donna attends clinic regularly and has a good relationship with her health visitor. The estate where the family lives has had problems with vandalism. Both Donna and her partner feel that the neighbours avoid them and Kylie has been subjected to racist taunts from other children. On balance the social worker decides that the best way to help the family is to link them up with local resources which will help Donna in her parenting of the younger children and give Kylie somewhere to go for social activities after school.

However this does not satisfactorily address all of the issues – Kylie's small stature and the reasons why her teacher felt concerned enough to refer her. Could it be that the family has not felt able to disclose all of their concerns – are they actively concealing factors which might cause the social worker to consider whether there is a need for further assessment? Let us suppose that the social worker does decide there is a need for a more extended assessment, a core assessment. She might still want the family to make use of local resources while that process is being completed – the family may be invited to attend a local family centre for the purposes of an assessment. (The core assessment will be discussed further in a later chapter). The social worker could also liaise with the education department over Kylie's difficulties in school. Are they just social problems or has she a learning difficulty? This could be ascertained by an assessment of Kylie's educational needs by an educational psychologist.

Partnership with the family

Throughout her contact with the family, the social worker will be striving to work in partnership with the family, to listen to their concerns, to consult them about the solutions that they think will work for their family. There is a difficult balance to be held between the rights and needs of the children and the rights and responsibilities of the parents. It is important not to forget Kylie's birth father Alan Cole, who although not living with Kylie does have regular contact with her and should also be consulted about any plans that might be made for Kylie. In the same way Ahmed Khan should be involved in discussions about Tariq and Nadia.

At this point the children are not considered to be at risk, and the relationship is one of voluntary support. The family may be ambivalent about having a social worker visit them at home, feeling that it indicates they are under surveillance. Donna may feel much more comfortable talking to the volunteer at the Sure Start playgroup, someone who has lived locally and brought up her children. The chance to talk about Tariq's demanding behaviour could be welcome, especially if the volunteer is able to suggest some strategies that might help Donna manage Tariq's behaviour more effectively. There may be the opportunity for Donna and Ahmed to attend a parenting programme, where again some of those leading the group may be parents who have had similar challenges in the past. Parenting programmes are provided for all ages, some are for parents of young offenders, who may be obliged to attend by a Parenting Order (Crime and Disorder Act 1998) for a period of three months for training and guidance.

There are a variety of parenting programmes used by centres providing support to families. Some are very structured and delivered by professionals; others are more informal and may be delivered by volunteers, or by professionals and volunteers working together. Some examples of parenting programmes that you may have heard of are the Webster-Stratton Parenting Programme, which was developed by Caroline Webster-Stratton, and the Mellow Parenting Programme developed by Christine Puckering, both of which have been extensively evaluated and use a variety of strategies to engage with parents and to help them learn new ways of interacting with their children. The Mellow Parenting Programme has been successful with very vulnerable families, nurturing the parents (usually single mothers) as well as promoting the development of the children. Some programmes such as Supporting Parents on Kids' Education (SPOKES) aim to improve relationships between parents and children by learning together. It is important to ask questions about the purpose of the programme before suggesting it to a family. Whilst all aim to improve relationships and promote children's development, the intensity or method may not be suitable for everyone. Some parents find attending groups daunting, in particular single parents with drug or alcohol problems and people with low self-esteem or who lack social skills may find a group unsatisfactory. There may be practical issues to consider. Will there be childcare available? Will the family have to travel? When is the session timed – can working parents get there, will there be men present? What provision is made for the older child?

C H A P T E R   S U M M A R Y

The chapter has looked at what we mean when we use the term 'family support' and explored some of the ways that our approach to family support has changed over time. We have looked at the role of the social worker in family support, considering the way legislation and policy have promoted preventive work, although there are often constraints on how this can be delivered. Currently there is an emphasis on supporting parents in the care of their children, with the New Labour interest in social investment, which has meant a significant shift in how services are structured and delivered to families with children. The concept of 'the child in need' has been considered and the response of Social Service Departments to children in need has been reviewed. We have looked at some of the ways that family support might be delivered, through Family Centres, Sure Start, and voluntary agencies such as Home Start and Newpin together with some of the programmes which are used in those centres.

FURTHER READING

Butt, J and Box, L (1998a) *Family centred: A study of the use of family centres by Asian families.* London: Race Equality Unit.
This book looks at the reasons why Asian families are under-represented in many family support settings.

Featherstone, B (2004) *Family Life and Family Support.* Basingstoke: Palgrave Macmillan.
This book takes a feminist perspective and considers how recent policy developments are impacting on family life.

Frost, N, Lloyd, A and Jeffrey, L (2003) *The RHP companion to family support.* Lyme Regis: Russell House Publishing.
This book, besides exploring theory and policy on family support has in Part Two accounts by practitioners of family support in action, and in Part Three a helpful guide to information sharing and networking to find out what services are available to support families.

Quinton, D (2004) *Supporting parents. Messages from research.* London: Jessica Kingsley Publishers.
This book presents in a readable form the recent government funded research which is guiding the development of current policy on family support.

Chapter 4

Working Effectively with Children and Families in the Safeguarding Children Arena

Julie Bywater

A C H I E V I N G   A   S O C I A L   W O R K   D E G R E E

This chapter will help you begin to meet the following National Occupational Standards:

Key Role 1: Prepare for and work with individuals, families, groups and communities to assess their needs and circumstances.
- Prepare for social work contact and involvement.
- Work with individuals, families, groups and communities to help them make informed decisions.
- Assess needs and options to recommend the course of action.

Key Role 2: Plan, carry out and review social work practice, with individuals, families, groups, communities and other professionals.
- Interact with individuals, families, groups, communities and professional colleagues.
- Work with individuals, families, groups and communities to identify, gather, analyse and understand information.
- Prepare, produce, implement and evaluate plans with individuals, families, groups, communities and professional colleagues.

Key Role 3: Support individuals to represent their needs, views and circumstances.
- Present evidence to, and help individuals, families, to be involved in decision-making forums.
- Enable individuals and families to understand the procedures in and outcomes from decision-making forums.

Key Role 4: Balance the rights and responsibilities of individuals, and families with associated risk.

Key Role 5: Manage and be accountable with supervision and support for your own social work practice within your own organisation.
- Manage and be accountable for your own work.

Key Role 6: Demonstrate professional competence in social work practice.
- Work within agreed standards of social work practice and ensure your own professional development

It will also introduce you to the following academic standards as set out in the social work subject benchmark statement:

2 Defining principles.

2.2.1 Social work is located within different social welfare contexts.

2.2.2 There are competing views in society at large on the nature of social work and on its place and purpose.

2.4 Social work is a moral activity that requires practitioners to make and implement difficult decisions about human situations that involve the potential for benefit or harm.

3.1.1. Social work services and service users.

- The social processes (associated with, for example, poverty, unemployment, poor health, disablement, lack of education and other sources of disadvantage) that lead to marginalisation, isolation and exclusion and their impact on the demand for social work services.
- The nature and validity of different definitions of, and explanations for, the characteristics and circumstances of service users and the services required by them.

3.1.2 The service delivery context.

- The issues and trends in modern public and social policy and their relationship to contempory practice and service delivery in social work.
- The significance of interrelationships with other social services, especially education, housing, health, income maintenance and criminal justice.

3.1.3 Values and ethics.

- The moral concepts of rights, responsibility, freedom, authority and power inherent in the practice of social workers as moral and statutory agents.

3.1.4. Social work theory.

The subject skills highlighted to demonstrate this knowledge in practice include:

- Research-based concepts and critical explanations from social work theory and other disciplines that contribute to the knowledge base of social work, including their distinctive epistemological status and application to practice.
- The relevance of psychological and physiological perspectives to understanding individual and social development and functioning.

5.2.1 Knowledge and understanding.

- Ability to use this knowledge and understanding in work within specific practice contexts.

Introduction

This chapter will focus on the skills and knowledge needed by social workers to work effectively with children and families within the safeguarding children arena. This arena which has for some years been referred to as 'child protection', is moving towards, in line with government policy, a new emphasis on 'safeguarding'. This term will be substituted for child protection within this chapter. The categories and definitions of child abuse will be briefly outlined with reference to the current guidance and suggested further reading. Particular reference will be given to the predominant factors currently being addressed by safeguarding practitioners throughout the country, specifically the impact of parental domestic violence, substance abuse and mental illness/distress in relation to children's development, welfare and safety (Cleaver, et al., 1999). Current legislation, policies, guidance and the framework for assessing children and families will be highlighted with examples for practice in relation to the Cole family case study.

Safeguarding a child from significant harm is a high profile area of social work practice. Every day many children of all ages in the UK experience physical, emotional, and sexual abuse as well as suffering neglect. It is estimated that between two and four children die every week as a result of abuse and/or neglect, with many more children suffering irreversible long-term effects (Barker and Hodes, 2007). What constitutes a concern about a child's welfare and whether it is child abuse, however, has been problematic to categorise and define throughout history. Social workers have frequently been faced with the dilemma of, on the one hand, safeguarding children from harm, for example by their parent/s (see for example the Jasmine Beckford Inquiry Report 1987), whilst on the other protecting the privacy and respect for family life from over-zealous state intervention, resulting at times in much criticism being directed at the individual social work practitioner (see for example the Cleveland Inquiry, 1988). The inquiry into the tragic death of Victoria Climbié, aged 8 years, in 2000 (Laming, 2003) from abuse and neglect, however, found that a range of professional networks had failed to act on concerns about her safety and welfare, and concluded that 'child protection is everyone's business'.

In response to the Victoria Climbié Inquiry, the Government published practice guidance to assist practitioners to work together to safeguard children from harm and promote their welfare (DoH, et al., 2003). Social workers, the police and health workers take the lead responsibility for the procedures and processes that protect children from harm, but in order to do so they all rely on others who know the child – for example, parent/s, nursery staff, teachers, child minders, family members, neighbours and so on in order to safeguard children from harm. Effective joint working and shared responsibility between the professionals and agencies involved is therefore required if children are to be safeguarded from harm and their welfare promoted (DfES, 2006, p10).

The current legislative and practice context of safeguarding children

Current legislation and practice guidance has been informed from a number of important publications including relevant research findings and Government guidance, and as highlighted in chapter 2, it is important that we are aware of these to understand and develop 'best' practice in this area.

In 2000 the Department of Health launched *Quality Protects: Framework for Action* (DoH, 1999). Within this, Objectives 2 and 7 are the most pertinent to child protection:

- Objective 2 – protecting children from abuse and neglect by reducing the number of deaths of children where abuse or neglect is a factor; reducing the incidence of child abuse and making sure that as few children as possible suffer from repeated abuse.

- Objective 7 – better assessment leading to better services by completing the initial assessment within seven working days, and by completing a core assessment within 35 days of the initial assessment.

In 1999, *Working Together to Safeguard Children – A Guide to Inter-Agency Working to Safeguard and Promote the Welfare of Children* was published which updated the original *Working Together* guidance in 1991, with a further two documents being supplemented, *Safeguarding Children Involved in Prostitution* (2000) and *Safeguarding Children in Whom Illness is Fabricated or Induced* (2002). These have continued to take effect alongside the new *Working Together* (2006), which has been updated in line with the *Children Act 2004* and other developments since (1999). To accompany the *Working Together* (1999) guidance the earlier publication (often referred to as the 'Orange Book') on assessment, *Protecting Children: A Guide for Social Worker's Undertaking a Comprehensive Assessment* (DoH, 1998) was replaced by the *Framework for Assessment of Children in Need and their Families* (DoH, 2000), this new guidance being relevant for all assessments, whether for children in need or for children at risk of significant harm where statutory intervention may be required.

The Children Act Now: Messages from Research (DoH, 2001) built upon the earlier messages from the research document of 1995 (see Chapter 2), and highlighted the importance of an *effectively integrated children's system for assessment and care planning* of children and families, incorporating an inter-agency approach to the assessments and interventions into children's lives, whilst also taking into account the wishes and feelings of the child.

The current legal framework for intervention in the area of safeguarding children continues to be largely contained in the Children Act 1989, but practice must also now be considered within the context of *Every Child Matters: Change for Children's Policy*, which incorporates the Common Assessment Framework (CAF) (which supplements the Framework for Assessment (2000)) and the legislative changes introduced by the Children Act 2004. The CAF provides a common approach to needs assessment and can be used by all professionals. Effective use of the CAF should lead to earlier holistic identification of children's needs; fewer assessments of individual children, and referral to specialists and local safeguarding children's teams (Brammer, 2006).

The Children Act 2004 is a major piece of legislation, shaping child care law, practice and policy to secure improvement in outcomes for children and young people. The Act (2004) does not introduce a range of new safeguarding powers, but does set the foundations for good practice in the use of existing powers contained in the Children Act 1989 through a holistically integrated approach to child care. The Children Act 2004 was implemented following the death of Victoria Climbié and the subsequent green paper, *Every Child Matters* (2003), which was later followed by the *Keeping Children Safe – Government's response to the Victoria Climbié Inquiry Report* (2003); the *Every Child Matters: Next Steps* (DfES, 2004) agenda, which covers all aspects of safeguarding the well-being of children through the development of more effective and accessible services focused around the needs of children, young people and their families, and the Joint Chief Inspectors Report, *Safeguarding Children*. In addition, the *National Service Framework for Children, Young People and Maternity Services* was published (DfES/DoH, 2004).

Duty to Investigate Concerns Regarding Children at Risk of Significant Harm

The Children Act 1989 section 47 (1) places a duty on local authorities to investigate where a local authority:

(a) is informed that a child who lives, or is found, in their area:
   (i) is the subject of an emergency protection order; or
   (ii) is in police protection, section 46; or
(b) has reasonable cause to suspect that a child who lives, or is found, in their area is suffering, or is likely to suffer, significant harm,
(c) the authority shall make, or cause to be made, such inquiries as they consider necessary to enable them to decide whether they should take any action to safeguard or promote the child's welfare (Children Act 1989).

Definitions and concepts

The Children Act 1989 introduced the concept of significant harm as the threshold that justifies compulsory intervention in family life in the best interests of children, and a Court may make a care order or supervision order in respect of a child if it is satisfied that

• the child is suffering, or is likely to suffer, significant harm; and

• the harm, or likelihood of harm, is attributable to a lack of adequate parental care or control (section 31).

A 'child' refers to anyone who has not reached their eighteenth birthday (Children Act(s) 1989 and 2004), so although 'child' is used throughout, it applies to both children and young people.

In *Every Child Matters* five outcomes for children's services were introduced:

• be healthy;

• stay safe;

• enjoy and achieve;

• make a positive contribution; and

• achieve economic well-being.

The Children Act 2004 included these outcomes, in slightly different wording, as areas for improving the well-being of children in section 10(2), relating to:

• physical and mental health and emotional well-being;

• protection from harm and neglect;

• education, training and recreation;

• the contribution made by them to society; and

• social and economic well-being.

Section 11 of the Act further imposes the duty to make arrangements to safeguard and promote welfare on a wide range of bodies, including for example; a children's service authority; district council; Primary Care Trust; NHS Trust; police authority; probation board; youth offending team; etc. (see s11(1) for others listed). Inter-agency working is the focus of this section and the duty to safeguard and promote the welfare of children is broader than preventing child abuse or responding to children in need, in that it is defined as

> *protecting children from maltreatment, preventing impairment of children's health or development; ensuring that children are growing up in circumstances consistent with the provision of safe and effective care; and undertaking that role so as to enable those children to have optimum life chances and to enter adulthood successfully* (section 11, para.2.8 Children Act 2004).

Alongside the Children Act 2004, several volumes of guidance were issued, including for example:

- Interagency co-operation to improve the wellbeing of children;

- Duty to make arrangements to safeguard and promote the welfare of children;

- *Working Together to Safeguard Children* (DfES, 2006) – which incorporates an important additional chapter on Local Safeguarding Children Boards.

Working Together to Safeguard Children (DfES, 2006) asserts that compulsory intervention into family life should take place when it is necessary to safeguard a child from significant harm. In such cases, all interventions (if consistent with the safety and welfare of the child) should include support for the families and assist them in developing plans to promote the welfare and protection of their child(ren).

To meet these requirements professionals involved will need to follow and adhere to the guidance provided in the new *Working Together to Safeguard Children* (DfES, 2006) and the *Framework for Assessment of Children in Need and their Families* (DoH, 2000), which incorporates the theoretical frameworks and underpinning knowledge base of child development, parenting capacity and the environmental factors that impact upon children's needs and safety. This ecological approach has been central in informing policy and provides an analysis to be made of the key risk factors that are likely to have an adverse effect on children's development and the corresponding protective factors that may help children to develop the resilience they will require if they are to thrive in relation to the outcomes listed in *Every Child Matters* (DfES, 2003, Scott and Ward, 2005).

The categories and definitions of abuse

ACTIVITY 4.1

Make a list of the following:

What do you think constitutes child abuse ?

Can you think of some of the types/categories and definitions of child abuse?

Who do you think are the main abusers of children?

Comment

Somebody may abuse or neglect a child by inflicting harm, or by failing to act to prevent harm. Children may be abused in a family or in an institutional community setting; by an adult or adults; or another child or children; by those known to them, by those who work with them in any and every setting by a professional, staff member, foster carer or volunteer or, more rarely, by a stranger.

(Working Together to Safeguard Children 2006 (1.29))

The most commonly agreed types of abuse are: emotional, physical and sexual abuse and neglect. These categories are used to define abuse, in Child Protection Registers.

Other forms of abuse, however, are also recognised, for example:

- Children abused/involved in prostitution and other forms of commercial sexual exploitation (these children may also be victims of human trafficking – see www.crimereduction.gov.uk/toolkits for further reading/guidance. The Home Office and Department of Health jointly published guidance in May 2000 on *Safeguarding Children Involved in Prostitution*).

- Concerns may also be raised when a child's health or development is considered to be significantly or further impaired by a parent/caregiver who has fabricated or induced a child's illness (for further reading/guidance see *Safeguarding Children in Whom Illness is Fabricated or Induced,* 2002).

- Complex (organised or multiple) abuse – children may also be abused where there is organised and multiple abuse involving one or more abusers and a number of children, for example, across a family or community and within institutions such as residential schools and homes. The abusers may be using an institutional framework or position of authority to recruit children for abuse (for further reading/guidance see The Home Office and Department of Health 2002 guidance, *Complex Child Abuse Investigations: Inter-agency issues*).

- Female genital mutilation (FGM) is another category of abuse and refers to the procedures that include the removal of part or all of the external female genitalia, for cultural or other non-therapeutic reasons. The Female Genital Mutilation Act 2003 makes it an offence, for the first time, for UK nationals or permanent UK residents to carry out FGM abroad, or to aid, abet, counsel or procure the carrying out of FGM abroad, even in countries where the practice is legal. A local authority may exercise its powers under section 47 of the Children Act 1989 if it has reason to believe that a child has suffered, or is likely to suffer FGM (for further information see Home Office Circular 10/2004 available at www.homeoffice.gov.uk and Local Authority Social services Letter LASSL (2004)4, available at www.dfes.gov.uk).

- Forced marriage – is another factor for consideration and refers to a marriage conducted without the full consent of both parties and where duress is a factor. Refusal to go through with a forced marriage is linked to so-called 'honour crimes'. It is extremely dangerous for the individual and can include abduction and murder (for further reading/guidance see www.adss.org.ukpublications/guidance/marriage.pdf and www.homeoffice.gov.uk/comrace/race/forcedmarriage/index.html)

Working Together (DfES, 2006) provides the following descriptions of the four major types of abuse.

1. **Emotional abuse** is the persistent emotional maltreatment of a child such as to cause severe and persistent adverse effects on the child's emotional development. It may involve conveying to children that they are worthless or unloved, inadequate, or valued only in so far as they meet the needs of another person. It may feature age or developmentally inappropriate expectations being imposed on children. These may include interactions that are beyond the child's developmental capacity, as well as overprotection and limitation of exploration and learning, or preventing the child participating in normal social interaction. It may involve seeing or hearing the ill-treatment of another. It may involve serious bullying, causing children frequently to feel frightened or in danger, or the exploitation or corruption of children. Some level of emotional abuse is involved in all types of ill-treatment of a child, though it may occur alone (1.31, p.38).

2. **Physical abuse** may involve hitting, shaking, throwing, poisoning or scalding, drowning, suffocating, or otherwise causing physical harm to a child (1.30, p.37).

3. **Sexual abuse** involves forcing or enticing a child or young person to take part in sexual activities, including prostitution, whether or not the child is aware of what is happening. The activities may involve physical contact, including penetrative (e.g. rape, buggery or oral sex) or non-penetrative acts. They may include non-contact activities, such as involving children in looking at, or in the production of, sexual online images, watching sexual activities, or encouraging children to behave in sexually inappropriate ways (1.32, p.38).

4. **Neglect** is the persistent failure to meet a child's basic physical and/or psychological needs, likely to result in the serious impairment of the child's health or development. Neglect may occur during pregnancy as a result of maternal substance abuse. Once a child is born, neglect may involve a parent or carer failing to:

    – provide adequate food, clothing and shelter (including exclusion from home or abandonment);

    – protect a child from physical and emotional harm or danger;

    – ensure adequate supervision (including the use of inadequate care-givers);

    – ensure access to appropriate medical care or treatment.

It may also include neglect of, or unresponsiveness to, a child's basic emotional needs (1.33, p.38).

The concept of harm

The Children Act 1989 introduced the concept of significant harm as the threshold to justify compulsory intervention in family life, to uphold the best interests of the child.

Make a list of what you understand by the following terms:

'harm'

'significant harm'.

Can you think of any examples that would equate to the term 'significant harm'?

Comment

Unfortunately, there is no absolute definition to rely upon when trying to judge/assess what constitutes as significant harm. *Working Together to Safeguard Children* (2006) states that:

> *consideration of the severity of ill-treatment may include the degree and the extent of physical harm, the duration and frequency of abuse and neglect, the extent of premeditation, and the presence or degree of threat, coercion, sadism and bizarre or unusual elements. Sometimes, a singly traumatic event may constitute significant harm, e.g. a violent assault, suffocation or poisoning. More often,* significant harm *is a compilation of significant events, both acute and long-standing, which interrupt, change or damage the child's physical and psychological development. Some children live in family and social circumstances where their health and development are neglected. For them, it is the long-term emotional, physical or sexual abuse that causes impairment to the extent of constituting significant harm. In each case, it is necessary to consider any maltreatment alongside the family's strengths and supports.* (p.36)

Under section 31(9) of the Children Act 1989 (as amended by the Adoption and Children Act 2002):

- *'harm' means ill treatment or the impairment of health or development, including, for example, impairment suffered from seeing or hearing the ill-treatment of another;*
- *'development' means physical, intellectual, emotional, social or behavioural development;*
- *'health' means physical or mental health; and*
- *'ill-treatment includes sexual abuse and forms of ill-treatment which are not physical.*

Under section 31(10) of the Act:

> *Where the question of whether harm suffered by a child is significant turns on the child's health and development, his health or development shall be compared with that which could reasonably be expected of a similar child.*

An excellent diagram is provided by Johns (2007) page 68 to demonstrate the threshold criteria for significant harm.

Working openly and in partnership with parents in order to gain their involvement and participation is one of the underlying principles of the Children Act 1989. Parents have a central role in their children's welfare and protection from harm, and should therefore be included in all decisions and actions taken by professionals, wherever possible, when they have concerns about a child. In order to prevent and protect children from abuse, professionals need to help the child's parents provide good enough care of their children. In addition, *Working Together* (DfES 2006) requires local authorities to refer parents to independent advice and advocacy as soon as inquiries commence under section 47 (Children Act 1989).

If a parent or child is disabled, they may also require additional support with communication in order for them to fully participate; interpreters should also be provided for those whose first language is not English. It is also important that professionals ascertain the wishes and feelings of the child, in cases where the age and development of children limits their level of understanding; their wishes and feelings will need to be judged as far as possible through direct observations of the child (DfES, 2006, para. 5.63). Para. 5.64 of *Working Together* (DfES, 2006) highlights the importance of talking to children:

> *children are a key, and sometimes the only, source of information about what has happened to them, especially in sexual abuse cases.*

Sensitivity is required when interviewing children and para. 5.64 (DfES, 2006) further points out that:

> *children may need time, and more than one opportunity, in order to develop sufficient trust to communicate any concerns they may have.*

When inquiries are being made within the context of section 47, the local authority must take steps to obtain access to the child (s.47(4) Children Act 1989), and if access is denied or the local authority is denied information as to the child's whereabouts, the local authority may need to apply for an emergency protection order, or other appropriate order (section 37, Children Act 1989), unless the local authority are satisfied that the child's welfare can be satisfactorily safeguarded without doing so (section 47(6) Children Act 1989).

Emergency protection powers

There are a range of powers available to Local Authorities and others such as the NSPCC and the police if required to take emergency action to safeguard children.

1. The court may make an emergency protection order under s44 of the Children Act 1989, if it is satisfied that there is reasonable cause to believe that a child is likely to suffer significant harm if:
   (a) s/he is not removed to different accommodation; or
   (b) s/he does not remain in the place in which s/he is then being accommodated.

   An emergency protection order may also be made if enquiries (e.g. made under s47) are being frustrated by access to the child being unreasonably refused to a person authorised to seek access, and the applicant has reasonable cause to believe that access is needed as a matter of urgency. An emergency protection order gives authority to remove a child, and places the

---

child under the protection of the applicant, who then also acquires parental responsibility (s.44(4) c)) which is limited to what is necessary to safeguard the welfare of the child. During the order, the child must be able to have reasonable contact with his/her parents or with whom the child was living immediately before the order, subject to any specific directions given by the court. If it appears safe during the order the local authority may return the child home, however, if circumstances change the child can be removed again (s.44 (12)). An emergency protection order lasts for eight days but it is possible to be extended, once only, for a further seven days.

The court may also include an exclusion requirement in an interim care order or emergency protection order (Sections 38A and 44A of the Children Act 1989).This allows a perpetrator to be removed from the home instead of having to remove the child. The court however, must be satisfied that:

(a) there is reasonable cause to believe that if the person is excluded from the home in which the child lives, the child will cease to suffer, or cease to be likely to suffer, significant harm, or that enquires will cease to be frustrated; and

(b) another person living in the home is able and willing to give the child the care that it would be reasonable to expect a parent to give, and consents to the exclusion requirement.

2. Under s46 of the Children Act 1989, where a police officer has reasonable cause to believe that a child would otherwise be likely to suffer significant harm, s/he may:

(a) remove the child to suitable accommodation and keep him or her there; or

(b) take reasonable steps to ensure that the child's removal from any hospital, or other place in which the child is then being accommodated is prevented.

A child may only be kept in police protection however, for 72 hours (Brammer, 2006).

In the event of an order being sought/made in respect of a child the court will allocate a children's guardian (appointed by CAFCASS, section 12 Criminal Justice and Court Services Act 2000) to the child who will ascertain their wishes and feelings and present these to the court through a comprehensive report (Johns, 2007).

The assessment framework and legislation (specifically relating to safeguarding children)

The Framework for the Assessment of Children in Need and their Families provides for a systematic assessment of children and their families. The Framework embraces three key areas/dimensions: the child's developmental needs; parenting capacity; and the wider family and environmental factors. The aim of the assessment is to identify and clarify the needs of the child in relation to their overall development and safety and the parents ability to empathically understand and give priority to meeting the child's needs. An important component in addressing parenting capacity in the context of child abuse is to gain the parents understanding and acceptance of their behaviours/actions that have resulted in harm to the child. Jones (1997) points out that if parents do not acknowledge that their caring has been seriously compromised it may not be possible to begin the process of rectification, and the continuation of that particular parent-child relationship is likely to be untenable.

The checklist contained in the *Framework for Assessment of Children in Need and their Families* (DoH, 2000), known as the referral chart, is used as a starting point for information to be obtained and recorded at the initial referral stage (see an excellent example provided by Brammer, 2006, pp254–255).

Assessment of the child's/family's race and culture should also be addressed integrally, and consideration given to whether any racial/cultural stereotyping of Black or minority ethnic families have led to the intervention, or if there has been a failure to protect Black or minority ethnic children from abuse. Cohen (2003) highlights that issues of race can have a powerful impact on the choices that practitioners make:

> *Sometimes race and culture may lead to more intrusive interventions, but at other times, they seem to normalise unacceptable behaviour. The cultural and racial background of families influences the specific factors that workers consider in assessing the severity of risk and level of intervention. Decisions are more likely to be made on the basis of deficits in available resources, accepted agency practice, personal values and biases, and notions of an ideal family than by application of consistent case rules.* (p2)

It is important therefore for practitioners to differentiate between parenting practices that enhance a child's well-being and safety and those that are potentially harmful, and it is essential that all practitioners involved in child protection investigations develop an understanding and level of proficiency in working with a range of diverse cultures, and to develop an understanding of their own cultural identity and attitudes. An understanding of how the impact of oppression, prejudice and discrimination and the influences these have on cultural biases and stereotypes is very important to demonstrate culturally responsive practice (Connolly, et al., 2006). Practitioners must also be aware that child abuse and neglect exists within all cultures and communities, and if cultural and religious factors are accepted as offering an explanation for abuse, it could increase the risk of greater harm for some children. Practitioners must therefore avoid colluding with abuse and challenge, sensitively, any behaviour that is being perceived as harmful (Barker & Hodes, 2007).

The Framework for Assessment has specific timescales for the completion of assessments following a request/referral to social services (see Fig 4.1).

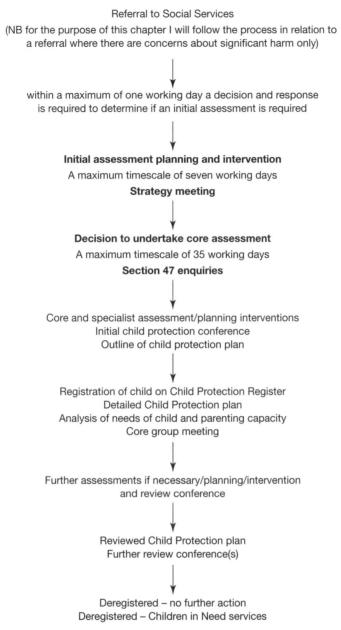

Referral to Social Services
(NB for the purpose of this chapter I will follow the process in relation to
a referral where there are concerns about significant harm only)

within a maximum of one working day a decision and response
is required to determine if an initial assessment is required

Initial assessment planning and intervention
A maximum timescale of seven working days
Strategy meeting

Decision to undertake core assessment
A maximum timescale of 35 working days
Section 47 enquiries

Core and specialist assessment/planning interventions
Initial child protection conference
Outline of child protection plan

Registration of child on Child Protection Register
Detailed Child Protection plan
Analysis of needs of child and parenting capacity
Core group meeting

Further assessments if necessary/planning/intervention
and review conference

Reviewed Child Protection plan
Further review conference(s)

Deregistered – no further action
Deregistered – Children in Need services

Figure 4.1 *Timescale for assessment*

Source: DoH (2000) *Framework of assessment for children in need and their families*. The Stationery Office.

In addition to the timescales set by the Framework in relation to the Initial and Core
Assessments, Child Protection procedures also have set timescales (see Fig 4.2).

Referral
S.47 Investigation

↓

Child Protection conference
within 15 days

↓

Is the child at continuing risk of significant harm?
Registration

↓

Physical/emotional/sexual/abuse/neglect

↓

Key worker/core group

↓

Core Assessment
within 42 days

↓

Review
within three months and thereafter every six months
for as long as the child remains on the register

Figure 4.2 *Safeguarding children procedures timescales*

Source: DoH (2000) *Framework of assessment for children in need and their families*. The Stationery Office.

Excellent diagrams are also provided in *Working Together* (DfES, 2006) see pages 142–146.

The rest of the chapter gives a brief overview of the procedures and requirements involved at each stage.

1. Referral to social services

Referrals raising concerns about children's welfare are received by local authorities from a variety of sources, for example:

- Other professionals (e.g. GPs, health visitors, teachers, etc.) who have a legal duty (s47 of the Children Act 1989) to report concerns and help the local authority with its enquiries).

- Members of the public (e.g. the child/young person themselves, family members, neigh-bours). There is no legal obligation for this group to report concerns.

In the majority of situations, social worker's provide a reactive rather than a proactive service in child protection situations as they rarely witness situations themselves where the abuse is taking place. Almost all referrals will require some level of investigation but a relatively small number of these will go on to court proceedings.

Sometimes whilst working with service users in other settings, for example, working with adults or young people in drug and alcohol services, mental health services and youth offending teams, social workers will encounter new information that raises their concern about the welfare of a child. In these situations the worker should discuss these concerns with the service user, and where possible, seek their agreement to make a referral to the children and family team. However, in certain situations caution maybe needed when discussing the concerns, and seeking agreement with the service user may result in the child being placed at increased risk of significant harm. The welfare of the child is paramount. Information should therefore be conveyed to the safeguarding team that the service user has not been informed of the referral (DfES, 2006).

If a referral constitutes, or may constitute, a criminal offence against a child the police should be automatically informed. This will enable both agencies to consider jointly how to proceed, whilst maintaining the best interests of the child. Where there are offences against a child, social services and the police will work in partnership during the initial enquiries. It is the responsibility of the police to instigate criminal proceedings but in less serious cases it is usually agreed that the best interests of the child are served by interventions led by social services rather than a full police investigation (DfES, 2006).

(a) **Receiving a referral** as the social worker on duty responding to incoming referrals, it is important that you check and correctly record concerns about a child with the person making the referral: what is the nature of the concerns?; and how have they arisen? If the referral is made by another professional they should follow their referral up in writing.

(b) **Within the first working day** clarity about any action to be taken, by whom and all decisions made will be recorded in writing by the relevant team manager. A referral at this stage can lead to no further action, or, to the provision of support and/or, to further investigations, with the possibility of seeking to obtain an emergency order to safeguard the child.

(c) **A strategy discussion** with social services, the police, health or other agencies as appropriate will be held following a referral about a child who is perceived to be at risk of significant harm. *A decision to undertake a core assessment/section 47 enquiries* will then be made to undertake further investigations and instigate any short-term emergency actions as required. Decisions will be agreed between the referrer and the relevant manager in line with the Working Together (DfES, 2006) and Local Safeguarding Children Board procedures about what the child's parent/s will be told, by whom and when.

The child protection practitioner and any other professionals already involved with the child will begin to work together at this point, for example health visitor, midwife, GP, teachers, school nurse, community mental health, drug/alcohol specialists, etc. establishing the core group. Lead responsibility for action to safeguard and promote the child's welfare will lie with social services. However, in all cases where the police are involved, the decision about when to inform the parents (about referrals from third parties) will have a bearing on the conduct of police investigations.

As part of the initial investigations, records held by social services, NSPCC, health, education, police and probation services will be checked to establish if any of the family members/adults involved with the child have had any previous involvement with any of the agencies, and if any criminal convictions or allegations of offences against a child have been recorded. In Britain, police checks reveal if any member of the household has been convicted of serious crimes against children (these are termed 'Schedule 1 Offences' under the Children and Young Person's Act 1933, which set out a list of offences against children and young people. The term 'schedule 1 offender' has subsequently come into wide use to describe anyone convicted of an offence against a child, and is a label that lasts for life. The presence of a 'schedule 1 offender' within the home environment of a child has normally triggered an assessment of risk by social services. The term 'risk to children' has now been adopted for those people who have been identified as posing an ongoing risk to a child – see local authority social services letter (LASSL): 'Identification of individuals who present a risk to children' for further clarification. If it becomes apparent that the family are known to have had regular contact with any other agencies (for example, police, probation, housing, the NSPCC) then relevant information from their records will also be requested. Section 47 (9) of the Children Act 1989 and sections 10 and 11 of the Children Act 2004, provides for a range of organisations to make arrangements to assist the local authority in their enquiries with regard to the need to safeguard and promote the welfare of children (Brammer, 2006).

In cases of suspected significant harm, for example physical and/or sexual abuse, an experienced qualified social worker will arrange to see and interview the child(ren), and will therefore need to obtain access to the child(ren) and seek the parents permission to do so. If access is denied by the child's parents a child can be removed and a safe placement with a relative or local authority foster carer would be sought by applying for an emergency protection order as previously listed, unless they are satisfied that the child can be satisfactorily safeguarded without doing so (see Section 47 (6)) of the Children Act 1989). Emergency intervention to remove the child from the family environment can also be instigated at any time during the core assessment/section 47 enquiry timescales and processes.

If a criminal prosecution is likely to be brought against the perpetrator of the abuse, guidance as to the conduct of investigative interviews is contained in *Achieving Best Evidence in Criminal Proceedings: Guidance for Vulnerable or Intimidated Witnesses including Children* (Home Office, 2001), which replaced the *Memorandum of Good Practice on Video Recorded Interviews with Child Witnesses for Criminal Proceedings* (HMSO, 1992). The interview will be carried out jointly by officers from the police and social services who have undertaken specialist training. The guidance also extends to pre-trial witness support and preparing the child for the court hearing. The guidance includes general principles for interviewing children, including for example, establishing a rapport with the child; ascertaining the child's understanding of truth and lies; establishing the purpose of the interview; raising issues of concern; obtaining a free narrative account; any further questions and closure. The Youth Justice and Criminal Evidence Act (1999) make further provision in the form of 'special measures' (s.16) relating to the evidence of vulnerable and intimidated witnesses, including children. Special measures include, for example: use of screens so that the child cannot see the accused (s.23); giving evidence by live link (s.24); removal of wigs and gowns while the child testifies (s.26); video recording of cross-examination and re-examination (s.28); giving evidence in private (in sexual offences cases), i.e. the press are removed (s.25); examination of witness through an intermediary – this could be an interpreter or person with particular communication skills or a social worker (s.29). The advantages for the child of these new measures, particularly the pre-recorded cross-examination videos, are that it is now possible for therapy to start earlier with the child, as the risks of contaminating evidence and undermining credibility will diminish (Brammer, 2006).

The core assessment/section 47 enquiry must be carried out properly and undertaken within 42 days of the initial referral being received (this incorporates 7 days for the initial assessment and 35 days for the core assessment). In some cases however, particularly for example, when paediatric/psychiatric assessment findings are awaited, an extension to this time frame will be required.

In cases of actual/alleged physical and sexual abuse and sometimes in the cases of neglect, a paediatrician will be contacted and arrangements made to undertake a full examination of the child(ren). This is undertaken in order to establish any health concerns in relation to the immediate medical needs of the child and to gather forensic evidence of abuse for legal proceedings. In physical abuse cases, the medical examination will normally be undertaken by a hospital paediatrician as soon after the abusive event as possible. In child sexual abuse cases the examination may be undertaken by a police surgeon. Forensic evidence in child sexual abuse cases needs to be gathered as soon as possible, often within 72 hours of the last occasion of abuse. The child has the right to refuse examinations, and the parent also has the right to refuse on their behalf, in some circumstances. In practice however this seldom occurs.

If emergency protection orders are authorised, the local authority Looked After Children and Substitute Care social work teams (see Chapter 6) will be notified of the possible emergency accommodation of the child(ren), and appropriate placement with wider family members will also be pursued. Placements will need to take account of the child(ren)'s ethnicity and cultural background.

CASE STUDY

A referral is made to social services by the school nurse involved with Kylie Cole. Kylie is 12 years old, she is of African-Caribbean/White heritage, and has learning disabilities. The nurse states that she has had growing concerns about Kylie over the past few weeks, she is not mixing well with other children, and her teachers have commented that her behaviour in class over the past couple of months has become more disruptive and difficult to manage. Kylie went to the nurse this morning complaining of stomach pains. When the nurse examined Kylie, she was concerned about how thin and emaciated she appeared, she was dirty and smelly, her skin was very dry, cracked and sore, she had severe and extensive new and old bruising and bite marks to her chest, inner thighs and buttocks. Upon weighing her Kylie has lost 2 stones in weight since starting at the school nine months ago. The nurse adds that Kylie appeared frightened and would not comment on how the bruising might have happened.

The nurse has not informed Kylie's mother, Donna Green, of the referral. Kylie's father, Alan Cole (who no longer lives with Kylie and her mother), usually collects Kylie from school, but is currently on holiday abroad and not expected back until next week. Kylie lives with her mother, her mother's partner Ahmed Khan who is Asian, and their children Tariq aged 3 years, and Nadia aged 1 who both have African-Caribbean and Asian dual heritage. The nurse also reports the school have tried to discuss their concerns in the past many times, and again last week about Kylie's behaviour – with her father in person, and her mother by letter – but were met with little or no response/concern.

ACTIVITY 4.3

From the information in the case study and your reading so far:

- *What do you think the categories of abuse are?*

- *How would you categorise the concerns in relation to the criteria for initiating a section 47 enquiry?*

- *What do think has been happening to Kylie?*

- *How does this information make you feel?*

- *How do you think you would respond to Kylie's mother, her mother's partner, and her father?*

Comment

From the information available at this time, it would appear that Kylie is suffering from neglect and possibly also emotional, physical and/or sexual abuse. The history of the school's and nurse's concerns would indicate that these issues have been long-standing, and could therefore be assessed in the category of 'significant harm'. As Kylie is presenting with the appearance of being emaciated and with extensive bruising and bite marks an immediate strategy discussion would be held, and a section 47 enquiry established. The police would be notified and checks on all of the adults involved with Kylie would be undertaken, to find out if there had been any previous involvement with any of the agencies, as well as any previous criminal convictions or allegations of offences against a child.

A safeguarding children social worker will need to arrange to see and interview Kylie and will need to obtain access to her. If access is denied by Kylie's mother, the local authority could apply for an emergency protection order unless they are satisfied that Kylie can be satisfactorily safeguarded without their doing so (see Section 47 (6)).

At this stage the local authority would advise Kylie's parents to contact independent legal advice and an advocacy agency. A criminal investigation may need to be conducted, and so a joint approach to interviewing Kylie may be appropriate as previously highlighted. A paediatrician/police surgeon would also be contacted, and arrangements made to undertake a full examination of Kylie and, possibly, her siblings, to establish any specific medical concerns/treatment and obtain forensic evidence of any possible abuse.

The paediatric assessment will form part of the jigsaw that will make up the whole picture by adding to the information that will be gathered from Kylie, her parents and the professionals involved during the core assessment process. The paediatric assessment may confirm any suspicions of non-accidental injuries, neglect or sexual abuse, and if necessary provide evidence for care or criminal proceedings. The assessment could also identify any underlying medical problems that could be causing the signs or symptoms of abuse and neglect, and provide follow-up medical support to monitor any deterioration in Kylie's health that may arise from her injuries, or in the case of sexual abuse, if she has contracted any infections.

How did you think you would feel? Were you surprised by any of the feelings that the case study raised for you?

Working with children in situations like this raises emotive feelings and reactions. You will need to know what kinds of situations you find most difficult and which you find easier to deal with. By understanding feelings that may arouse a desire to 'rescue' children and knowing what kinds of parental actions make you feel punitive is crucial in child protection work. You need to be aware of how your feelings and reactions could influence your judgement of the situation and the needs of others. Feelings of anger may motivate social workers involved in safeguarding children to work hard for the child, but anger can also cloud their judgment and make it more possible for mistakes to be made. Sometimes the reactions to abuse can result in some professionals being intimidating, cold and rejecting towards parents and other professionals. Being respectful of parents is not, however, incompatible with making the child's needs paramount, and failing to recognise and respect the importance of parents and family for a child would be to ignore one of the child's most basic needs. Sometimes even abusive and neglectful parents love their child and see themselves as the protector of the child. It is also important to remember that in the majority of cases, children will not be removed from their families. Social workers will therefore need to build an alliance with the child's parents and family to promote and maintain the safety and welfare of the child.

Social workers may also try and avoid the painful or frightening responses, witnessing the distress of a seriously abused child may be very difficult to bear and can result in avoiding interventions that need to be made; this can also be very dangerous in child protection work. Fear is another major feature of child protection work, for example, fear of making a mistake; of being blamed; of anger and hostility of others; and fear for your own safety when dealing with violent, threatening individuals. In the case of Jasmine Beckford (London Borough of Brent, 1985) who died as a result of physical abuse, for example, a social worker visited Jasmine's family several times when Jasmine was present but still managed to avoid noticing that Jasmine was suffering with several broken bones, *perhaps she could not bear to let herself see it* (Beckett, 2007, p49). A result of the responses highlighted can end up with professionals being preoccupied with protecting themselves as with protecting the child. Being aware of your own needs and addressing them openly and honestly in supervision is essential if you are to offer the best service to a child and their families (Beckett, 2007).

2. The core assessment

The core assessment provides a systematic basis for collecting and analysing information to support professional judgments about how to help children and families in the best interests of the child. A risk assessment in relation to the child's developmental needs; the capacity of the parents to respond appropriately to those needs – including the capacity to keep the child safe from harm; and the impact the wider family and environmental factors have on the parents and the child, are incorporated and analysed.

ACTIVITY **4.4**

Make a list of what you consider to be the developmental needs of children in relation to the following age groups:

0 – 2yrs; 3 – 4 yrs; 5 – 9yrs; and 10 – 14yrs.

Check your list as you read through the dimensions of the child's developmental needs. (You will refer back to this list in the next activity.)

Dimensions of the child's developmental needs

Child development theories are essential underpinning knowledge for social work practice within children's services, but in the area of safeguarding children, they are crucial. Understanding developmental milestones will provide generalised guidelines for undertaking assessments, refer to chapters 2, 3, 4 and 5 in Crawford and Walker (2007) *Social Work and Human Development*, second edition. Learning Matters for revision. The comprehensive checklists developed by Mary Sheridan in the Framework for Assessment Guidance (DoH, 2000) will also provide a helpful tool for practitioners.

The Framework for Assessment (DoH, 2000) identifies five dimensions of undertaking direct work with the child during assessments in order to obtain knowledge and an understanding of the child:

• seeing the child;

• observing them;

• engaging with them;

• talking with them; and

• doing activities with them.

(Bell and Wilson, 2003)

Working together, the allocated social worker with health and education professionals involved with the child (for example health visitor, GP, school nurse, paediatrician, designated teacher, child protection, educational psychologist) would undertake an assessment of the:

• Child's health

This would include their growth and development, as well as their physical and mental health wellbeing; the impact of disability and any genetic factors; if the child has received appropriate health care if needed in the past, an adequate and nutritious diet, immunisations, optical and dental care; whether the child or a family member may be likely to suffer sickle cell disorder; and whether past life experiences or trauma have had any detrimental affects on the physical health of the child. The extent to which the family have direct access to appropriate services and advice in relation to health care should also be considered. If the child is disabled or has an impairment – consideration of whether this has a direct effect on the child's growth, development and physical or mental wellbeing is required. It is also important to ascertain if there are any disabling barriers which limit the child or hinder their development (Horwath, et al., 2001; *Working Together*, 2006). Assessments of children with a disability should also include the question: *Would I consider that option if the child were not disabled? Clear reasons are necessary if the answer is no* (Middleton, 1996).

• Child's education

This would cover all areas of the child's cognitive development which begins from birth – focusing upon the opportunities provided for the child to play and interact with other children; have access to books and stimulating toys, etc. However, children's learning can also be encouraged in a range of different ways and the provision of toys is not a guarantee of a stimulating environment. Assessments of educational and cognitive development should also take account of racism, and address whether the child has the opportunity to realise their potential – without the limitations of negative stereotyping

• Child's emotional and behavioural development

This would address the appropriateness of responses demonstrated in feelings and actions by the child, initially to parents and, as the child is growing older, to others beyond the family. Assessments would address if the child is loved and/or valued for who they are; if they are listened to, and if their personal care is being undertaken respectfully. You will need to consider if there any concerns in relation to the child's emotional development. For example, is the child being treated in ways which are appropriate for their age and development, and what messages is the child receiving about their disability? If a child is seen to be unable to give or withhold their consent and is resisting any treatment/interventions – this will need to be acknowledged and addressed. It is important to assess if the child is supported in taking reasonable risks in every situation; if the acquisition of a positive racial identity has been considered, and have cultural and linguistic backgrounds of the child and family been fully taken into account. An observation and understanding of the pattern of attachment for this family in particular is essential – this may include attachment figures who are not necessarily birth relatives. The impact that migration, separation and trauma may have on the child and family as well as the nature and quality of the child's early attachments should also be acknowledged. The child's temperament, resilience and vulnerability factors, adaptation to change, and their response to stress and appropriate degree of self-control should also be assessed.

• Child's identity

This would focus upon the child's growing sense of self as a separate and valued person. The extent to which the child has the opportunity to learn/maintain their family language(s), and if any action is needed to support the child's identity development with regards to family and community life is required will include the child's view of themselves and their capabilities, self-esteem and self-image. Issues about their ethnicity, culture, religious beliefs, gender, sexuality and disability may all contribute to this. It is very important to ascertain if the child has feelings of belonging and being accepted by their family, peer group and the wider society.

• Child's family and social relationships

This would focus upon the child's development of empathy, and the capacity to place themselves in someone else's shoes. This would ascertain if the child's relationships with their parents or care providers, siblings, and friends were stable and affectionate for the child. Who are the important people in the child's life? What supports are available to help the family with their disabled child? Are any of the key adults aware of the increased vulnerability of disabled children to being abused? Are any family members/adults discriminating against the child due to their parentage? These are all important questions within this context.

• Child's social presentation

This would focus upon the child's growing understanding of the way in which appearance, behaviour and any impairment are perceived by the outside world and the impression being created. This would include the child's appropriateness of dress for age, weather conditions, gender, culture and religion, cleanliness and hygiene and the availability of advice from parents or caregivers about presentation in different settings.

• Child's self-care skills

This would focus upon the child's practical, emotional and communication competencies that are required for increasing their independence. This would include their early skills in dressing and feeding themselves, participating in activities away from the family environment as older children and using problem-solving approaches.

A brief review of the impact that parental mental health, substance abuse or domestic violence has on children's development

Infants aged 0–2 years

They may be damaged before birth (for example foetal alcohol syndrome); may be harmed or murdered by their parents, for example of all children who are killed or seriously injured

81 per cent have their injury caused by parents who are experiencing mental illness (Falkov, 1996). Infants may also be harmed if their parent's concentration is impaired because of drug or alcohol misuse or mental illness (for example depression), as the needs of the child for nourishment, nappy changes etc. are not met, they may be dressed inappropriately and their personal hygiene grossly neglected, or be in an unsafe environment (for example with used hypodermic needles, or in situations of domestic violence). An infant's cognitive development may be delayed through inconsistent, neglecting or under-stimulating behaviour. Babies may also be suffering with withdrawal symptoms from foetal addiction and be difficult to manage, a lack of commitment and increased unhappiness, tension and irritability in drug/alcohol using parents may result in inappropriate responses which can lead to faulty attachments. Depressed mothers may also be more irritable, tense, unhappy and disorganised and therefore interact with the infant less, or convey anger which may result in insecurely attached children. Some mothers experiencing violence from the child's father may also emotionally distance themselves from their children.

Children aged 3–4 years

They may be physically at risk from drugs and needles when they are left at home alone whilst their parents go out to buy alcohol/drugs, or left with unsuitable carers. Children may not be fed or provided with sufficient clothing due to the lack of money, as priority is focused upon buying drugs/alcohol. Children are at increased risk from parental mental illness if they are subjected to hostile and aggressive behaviour, neglected and/or experience rejection. Children's cognitive development may be delayed through parent's disorganisation and failing to attend pre-school facilities. Attachments may be damaged due to inconsistent parenting and children may learn inappropriate behavioural responses from witnessing domestic violence and display emotional symptoms similar to those of post-traumatic stress disorder. The impact of adverse parenting for this age group is more damaging – as the children may blame themselves for their parent's problems and being neglected. Children can also be affected if they have been the subject of their parent's delusions or hallucinations. They may also attempt to correct their parent's behaviour and try to put it right, believing themselves to be responsible, for example trying to protect their mother from domestic violence and sustaining injuries. Children may be left for periods of time with inappropriate adults and exposed to abuse. In peer settings children may have learnt to resolve conflict through violence and have problems establishing friendships with other children as a result. Children may be reluctant to form other attachments and relationships by believing they are in constant danger and by being unnaturally fearful and vigilant. Basic hygiene may be neglected and children may be left in a filthy condition, they may take on responsibilities beyond their years and abilities because of parental incapacity and be increasingly at risk as a result.

Children aged 5–9 years

They may have an increased risk of injuries and medical problems, many children develop psychosomatic problems relating to anxiety, for example headaches, stomach pain and discomfort, difficulty sleeping, and bedwetting as a result of domestic violence. Academic attainment is usually poor and the child's behaviour in school is often problematic, with low attendance etc. Children may show their distress by uncontrolled behaviour, emotional distress and fear. Children also have a higher rate of conduct disorder if their parents are suffering from depression. Children witnessing domestic violence have also shown problems in controlling their temper, emotions and behaviour. For some children, being the same gender as a parent who has problems appears to be more traumatising and psychologically distressing, resulting in a negative self-image and low self-esteem. They may have already developed anxiety and faulty attachments and therefore fear hostility and unplanned separations. Children may also feel embarrassed and ashamed of their parent's behaviour and curtail friendships and social interaction with their peer group. Children may experience shame and embarrassment if their clothing is inappropriate. They may be expected to take on too much responsibility for themselves and a caring role for their parent(s).

Young people aged 10–14 years

They risk having to cope with puberty without support; are at increased risk of psychological problems, neglect and physical abuse; and when living with parents with depression, young people can develop suicidal behaviour and depression. They may suffer increased anxiety due to their fear of being hurt when there is domestic violence or of being injured whilst trying to protect one parent from the other. Education is hampered by the young person's inability to concentrate and by missing school because of caring for siblings and/or parent(s). They may be at increased risk of emotional disturbance and conduct disorders, including bullying. There is an increased risk of sexual abuse in adolescent boys, whilst being in denial of their own needs and feelings. They may have a poor self-image and low self-esteem and blame themselves for their parent's problems and actions. The problems of being a young carer may also feel stigmatising and they may not receive any respect or praise for their efforts from their parent(s) or others. Relationships with parents are usually poor and they may fear exposing their family life to peers – and so restrict friendships. Many young people may resort to wandering the streets to avoid parental violence, go missing and sleep rough, and are more likely to become involved in crime and avoid school. Stigma may be acutely felt at this age because young people are self-conscious about their appearance and sensitive to how others perceive them. If they have learnt that violence is an accepted way of dealing with problems, they may use violent or aggressive means towards their peers and other adults, resulting in them becoming rejected and feeling alienated. They may be forced to assume too much responsibility for themselves and other family members, which may result in them failing to look after themselves and their own development needs (Cleaver, et al., 1999).

Teenagers aged 15 years and over

They are at greater risk of accidents; may have problems related to sexual relationships; may fail to achieve their potential; are at increased risk of school exclusion; have poor life chances due to exclusion and poor school attainment; have low self-esteem as a consequence of inconsistent parenting; experience increased isolation from both friends and adults outside the family; may use aggression inappropriately to solve problems; develop emotional problems that may lead to suicidal behaviour; have increased vulnerability to becoming involved in crime; sacrifice their own needs to meet those of their parents and siblings (Cleaver, et al., 1999).

> *If a child's development is optimal within their family, however deficient circumstances appear, family care is likely to be the best option for them.*
>
> (Petrie, 2003 cited in Bell and Wilson, 2003, p174)

> *The significance of seeing and observing the child throughout any assessment cannot be overstated.*
>
> (DoH, 2000)

ACTIVITY **4.5**

Make a list of what you consider to be the skills and qualities of a 'good' parent/caregiver.

Now try and match these lists up with your list of children's needs at their various stages of development.

Check your new list with your reading throughout the dimension of parenting capacity.

Dimensions of parenting capacity

For the assessment of parenting capacity good observation and analytical skills are crucial in order to gather the information required. A comparison can then be made in relation to the standards of good enough parenting.

Basic care

This involves assessing the parent's capacity to access and provide for the child's physical needs, their need for appropriate dental and medical care, including the provision of food, drink, warmth, shelter, clean and appropriate clothing and adequate personal hygiene.

Ensuring safety

This involves assessing the parent's capacity to ensure that the child is adequately protected from harm or danger; including their capacity to protect the child from significant harm or danger; preventing the child having contact with unsafe adults or other children and from self-harm. Parents should be able to demonstrate a recognition of the hazards and dangers both in the home and other places where the child spends time.

Emotional warmth

This involves assessing the parent's capacity to ensure that the child's emotional needs are met and give the child a sense of them being specially valued and a positive sense of their own racial and cultural identity. This will include the parent's capacity to ensure the child's requirements for secure, stable and affectionate relationships with significant adults are promoted with appropriate sensitivity and responsiveness to the child's needs, and that parents provide appropriate physical contact, comfort and cuddling sufficient to demonstrate warm regard, praise and encouragement.

Stimulation

This involves assessing the parent's capacity to promote a child's learning and intellectual development through encouragement and cognitive stimulation, by promoting social opportunities. This will include the parents or caregivers facilitating the child's cognitive development and potential through interaction, communication, talking and responding to the child's language and questions, encouraging and joining the child's play and promoting educational opportunities. Parents should be enabling the child to experience success and ensuring school attendance or equivalent opportunities, whilst also facilitating the child to meet the challenges of life.

Guidance and boundaries

This involves assessing the parent's capacity to enable the child to regulate his or her own emotions and behaviour. The key parental tasks are demonstrating and modelling behaviour; control of emotions and interactions with others; guidance which involves setting boundaries, so that the child is able to develop an internal model of moral norms and conscience, and social behaviour appropriate for the society within which s/he will grow up. The aim for the parent is to enable the child to grow into an autonomous adult, holding their own values and be able to demonstrate appropriate behaviour with others, rather than having to be dependent on rules outside themselves. This involves parents not being over-protective and enabling the child to explore and learn from their own experiences, thereby developing social problem-solving, anger management, consideration for others and effective self-discipline.

Stability

This involves assessing the parent's capacity to provide a sufficiently stable family environment to enable the child to develop and maintain a secure attachment to them in order to ensure the child's optimal development. This will include the parent's capacity to ensure secure attachments are not disrupted, provide consistency of emotional warmth over time and respond in a similar manner to the same behaviour of the child. It is also important that parents' and caregivers' responses change and develop according to the child's developmental progress, and in addition, that they ensure children keep contact with important family members and significant others.

Daniel, et al., (1999, Chapter 3) also provide brief summaries of some of the basic parenting tasks required for children of different age groups, and a table to help guide the assessment of parenting responses to children's needs at different stages is also provided on p50.

Summary of parenting/caregiving and child development

Children's needs can be met by several people, but there are aspects of parenting that are more helpful than others in enabling a child to reach their developmental milestones and potential. Daniel, et al., (2000) present some basic positive parenting tasks required for children in different age groups that can assist social workers in their interventions with parent/s to promote/improve their parenting capacity:

- **During infancy** developing a secure attachment between the parent and the child is of central importance and although the child is an active participant in this process of communication and interaction, it is principally in the control of the adult. Infants need parent(s) who can offer: overt control; attentiveness; warmth; stimulation; responsiveness and non-restrictive care.

- **During school age** children's lives should expand socially, emotionally and intellectually, therefore the parent will need considerable flexibility and responsiveness. The child needs: nurturing; encouragement of internalised control; increased use of induction and reasoning; encouragement with schooling; consistent discipline and expression of warmth.

- **During adolescence** adolescents require from their parent: empathy; parents who can see things from their point of view and offer constructive discipline not criticism and constraint; good communication and an active and warm involvement.

Appropriate non-stigmatising support from all involved practitioners has the potential to overcome some of the stresses of parenting and reduce the likelihood of abuse and neglect. Social workers need to assess and support the parents' ability to make use of the support that is available. Interventions needs to focus upon shifting the parents' perceptions of their own ability to change, assessing what is blocking their ability to use support and what therapeutic help is needed to overcome the block, for example using a motivational interviewing/solution focused approach, whilst helping the parent to step back and reflect on the quality of their relationship with the child. The main message that is helpful for both practitioners and parents is the importance of the combination of warmth and no criticism, with appropriate discipline and expectations (Daniel, et al., 1999).

Working with parents

All practitioners need to work in partnership with parents, and this involves a high level of interpersonal skills and a high degree of active participation from everyone involved. We will need to be able to ask difficult questions, for example asking a parent outright if they have punched/kicked their child. Some parents can be threatening/violent towards practitioners (as highlighted in *Messages from Research*, DoH, 1995a). This can be very frightening and result in practitioners avoiding questions that could provoke a violent response from the parent. All practitioners working with the child's family must ensure that they have due regard for their personal safety when working with parents whose violent behaviour raises child protection concerns, involving police officers in these situations can often be appropriate.

However, we also need to be mindful of not jumping to conclusions or assumptions, as examples of inaccurate judgments in cases where practitioners have pathologised parents by focusing on their deficiencies have resulted in the practitioners failing to understand and assess the whole overall situation, to the detriment of the child's needs (Munro, 1999). The pathologising of Black mothers is an example of the significant factors associated with the disproportionate representation of Black children in the child protection system, in cases of physical abuse and neglect. This incorporates the view that Black people, their lifestyles and culture are problematic and need correcting (Chand, 2000).

Caution must also be taken in relation to the practitioner over-empathising with the parent in their assessments, as neglect and abuse of the child can be overlooked. This is evidenced within the Laming Report (2003) following the death of Victoria Climbié, where guidance and legislation did not prevent Victoria's welfare becoming the secondary consideration for practitioners, whose main focus were her carers and their perceived/ assumed cultural practices.

Dimensions of the family and environmental factors

Any assessment needs to consider the wider context of the child including:

(a) **Family history and functioning** This includes genetic and psychosocial factors. An assessment is made of: how the family is functioning and influenced by the people living in the household; how these people relate to the child; if there have been any significant changes in the family/household composition; the parent's childhood experiences; a chronology of the significant life events and their meanings to family members; the nature of family functioning, including sibling relationships and their impact on the child; parental strengths and difficulties, including those of an absent parent; and the relationship between separated parents.

(b) **Wider family** It is important to ascertain who the child considers to be their family members, this may include related and non-related people. It is also important to ascertain what their role and importance to the child is.

(c) **Housing** An assessment will include: if the accommodation has the basic facilities and amenities appropriate to the age and development of the child and other people living there; if the housing is accessible and suitable to the needs of disabled family members; if the basic amenities include water, heating, sanitation, cooking facilities, sleeping arrangements and cleanliness, hygiene and safety, including the impact on the child's upbringing.

(d) **Employment** Who is working in the household, what patterns of work and any changes would be noted in relation to the impact this may have on the child, as would the family member(s)' views of work or the absence of work and how this affects relationships within the family.

(e) **Income** An assessment would include if there was a sufficient income to meet the family's needs, if there are any financial difficulties which could affect the child, if the family were in receipt of all available benefits and if the income is regular and sustained.

(f) **Family's social integration** An assessment would cover an exploration of the family's wider context in relation to their local neighbourhood and community and the impact that this may have on the child and parents/caregivers, the degree of the family's integration or isolation, their peer groups, friendship and social networks and the importance attached to them.

(g) **Community resources** An assessment would identify all facilities and services in the neighbourhood, including primary health care provisions, day care facilities and schools, places of worship, transport, shops and leisure activities, including the availability, accessibility and the standard of, or lack of, resources and the impact these may have on the family, including disabled family members.

Summary of research findings

As you can see from the core assessment dimensions presented, professionals working with children in the child protection arena will need to practise with full commitment to anti-oppressive practice by being aware of the impact of their own values in order to assess the child's needs holistically and by considering the impact that racism, gender, class, sexuality, disability, social exclusion and poverty have upon a parent's capacity to meet the child's needs.

Messages from Research (DoH, 1995, 2001) highlights the correlation between poverty and child maltreatment leading to child protection investigations. Understanding child abuse in these situations provides a systemic framework in which to conduct child protection practice and guide the practitioner in establishing supportive services to reduce situational stress that may be undermining parenting capacity, for example the services offered by the Sure Start programmes (see chapter 3). The provision of appropriate services should not wait until the end of the assessment process but should be determined according to what is required, and when, to promote the welfare and safety of the child.

Criticism has focused upon the failings of these structural mechanisms to address appropriately the needs of children from minority ethnic groups and those children with disabilities (Daycare Trust 2002/4 cited in Hill, 2004). Lawrence (2004) stresses that the most effective methods of managing child protection today are when practitioners also focus on the need to adopt a more culturally sensitive approach to child abuse and children's welfare generally.

The assessment process

As the investigation/assessment proceeds and information is gathered from all required sources as discussed, it is then assessed, measured and evaluated in relation to risk. All three dimensions of the core assessment are of equal focus and importance, as an overemphasis on any one may jeopardise the child's welfare. If significant harm is viewed as likely, that information is carried forward to the next stage of the process. If it is decided that there are no risks of significant harm, the child may then be referred as a 'child in need', to identify and implement any services that may still be required by the child and their family.

Specialist assessments involving a range of professionals (for example adult psychiatrists, community psychiatric nurses, community mental health social workers and drug agency workers) may be needed in a range of situations when there are serious concerns about a child's development being impaired through the impact of parental mental illness, drug or alcohol abuse, domestic violence, or learning disability. An identification of the family's supportive/protective networks needs to be identified, promoted and maintained. In some cases parents find it difficult explaining their inability to cope to their partner or other family members. This could be an important contributory factor in explaining severe and unexpected injuries to the child (Horwath, et al., 2001).

Throughout the assessment the professionals involved and the family should be working in partnership in trying to understand and address why the present concerns have arisen, or why they may arise again in the future. We also need to be constantly mindful of the stages involved in child development and avoid delays in assessment and interventions, as outcomes have the potential to affect the future. For example, lack of cognitive development in infancy due to neglect and lack of stimulation may result in poor academic performances in later childhood and successful outcomes to early interventions are likely to have a positive impact on a child and vice versa as an adult (Widom, 1991, cited in Horwath, et al., 2001). The assessment process also provides an opportunity for the family to reflect with the help of the worker, enabling them to develop and understand the explanations for concerns, and to develop improved coping strategies for possible solutions.

> ### *Messages for social workers undertaking a core assessment/section 47 enquiry*
>
> - Assessment time needs to be carefully planned.
>
> - Adequate time needs to be allocated to complete the work, with targets set for completion.
>
> - Clear and adequate recording is an essential component of a good assessment.
>
> - Assessment reports require a recognisable structure, should demonstrate the decision-making process which led to a specific plan and always be shared with the relevant parties.
>
> - Involve staff with specialist skills, including direct work with children.
>
> - The views of the children, families and carers should be clearly identified in all reports.
>
> Plans which follow an assessment of need should have clear objectives, timescales, details about the purpose of intervention, and the services to be provided, when and by whom.
>
> (Seden, et al., 2001)

3. Key process in safeguarding adults

The safeguarding (initial) conference

Within 15 days of the strategy discussion a safeguarding Conference will be convened. Working Together (DfES, 2006) states its purpose is to:

- *bring together and analyse in an interagency setting the information that has been obtained about the child's developmental needs, and the parents' or carer's capacity to respond to these needs to ensure the child's safety and promote the child's health and development within the context of their wider family and environment;*

- *consider the evidence presented to the conference, make judgments about the likelihood of a child suffering significant harm in future, and decide whether the child is at continuing risk of significant harm; and*

- *decide what future action is needed to safeguard the child and promote the welfare of the child, how that action will be taken forward, and with what intended outcomes,* (Working Together, 2006, p123)

Attendance

Para.5.82 *Working Together* (DfES, 2006, p124) points out that those attending the conference should be there because they have a significant contribution to make, arising from professional expertise, knowledge of the child or family or both. The local authority social work manager should consider whether to seek advice from, or have present, a medical professional who can present the medical information in a manner which can be understood by conference attendees and enable such information to be evaluated from a sound evidence base. There should be sufficient information and expertise available – through personal representation and written reports – to enable the conference to make an informed decision about what action is necessary to safeguard and promote the welfare of the child, and to make realistic and workable proposals for taking that action forward. At the same time, a conference that is larger than it needs to be can inhibit discussion and intimidate the child and family members. Those who have a relevant contribution to make may include:

- the child, or his/her representative;

- family members (including the wider family);

- LA children's social work staff who have led and been involved in an assessment of the child and family;

- foster carers (current or former);

- residential care staff;

- professionals involved with the child (e.g. health visitors, midwife, school nurse, children's guardian, paediatrician, school staff, early-years staff, the GP, NHS Direct);

- professionals involved with the parents or other family members (e.g. family support services, adult mental health services, probation, the GP, NHS Direct);

- Professionals with expertise in the particular type of harm suffered by the child or in the child's particular condition – e.g. a disability or long-term illness;

- Those involved in investigations (e.g. the police);

- LA legal services (child welfare);

- NSPCC or other involved voluntary organisations; and

- A representative of the Armed Forces, in cases where there is a service connection.

Before the conference is held, the purpose of the conference, who will be attending, and the way in which it will operate should always be explained to a child of sufficient age and understanding, and to the parents and involved family members. Where the child/family members do not speak English well enough to understand the discussions and express their views, an interpreter should be used (para.5.84 *Working Together*, DfES, 2006, p125).

1. **Introductions** during this stage each participant informs the conference who they are, which agency they belong to, and what contact they have had with the child and the child's family. If this stage is neglected, practitioners, the child, and the child's family will find it very difficult to understand and process the information being presented. Use of professional jargon/language should be avoided for the same reasons.

2. **Information sharing** this is the stage of the conference that takes up the most time. The specific incidents that led to the conference, and any further information obtained during the investigation/assessments by all involved practitioners, is presented verbally and by written reports in relation to the child and the child's family. These reports should be shared with the child and family prior to the conference. Information is powerful within this context and practitioners need to caution against information being exaggerated, minimised or withheld as the outcome of the conference may be seriously affected.

3. **Decisions and recommendations** this is the final stage of the conference where practitioners weigh up and consider all of the shared information and the personal accounts presented by the child and their family members. The conference should consider the following question when determining whether the child be the subject of a safeguarding plan:

Is the child at continuing risk of significant harm?

The test should be that either:

- The child can be shown to have suffered ill-treatment or impairment of health or development as a result of physical, emotional or sexual abuse or neglect, and professional judgement is that further ill-treatment or impairment are likely; or

- Professional judgement, substantiated by the findings of enquiries in this individual case or by research evidence, is that the child is likely to suffer ill-treatment or the impairment of health or development as a result of physical, emotional or sexual abuse or neglect (para.5.94, DfES, 2006, p128).

A decision as to whether or not to put the name of the child on the Safeguarding Children Register is then made in relation to the category of abuse defined (physical; emotional; sexual; neglect). A child could also be registered under more, or all of the categories of abuse in extreme cases. Each participant will be requested to offer their opinion on what the outcome of the conference should be.

If the conference is undertaken effectively the ability of the practitioners and parents to work together in partnership is enhanced, thus increasing the help and protection that is, and can be, offered to protect the child.

Safeguarding children

If the child is registered the conference will establish the key worker (a practitioner who will co-ordinate the case), which is usually the allocated social worker for the child.

Core group

A smaller inter-agency group of practitioners, joined by the child's parents, will then be allocated the responsibility for carrying out the child protection plan, which is established at the end of the conference. The core group are required to meet within ten days of the initial conference. Timescales for meetings and child protection plan reviews will be established.

The safeguarding plan

This will identify how the child is to be protected from harm, any outstanding assessments or enquiries still to be completed and in particular, identifying what needs to change in order to achieve the planned outcomes to safeguard and promote the welfare of the child. A contingency plan will be established to ensure an alternative protection plan is activated if agreed actions are not completed and/or circumstances change – e.g. if a care giver fails to achieve what has been agreed, a court application is not successful or a parent removes the child from a place of safety.

Review safeguarding Conference

A date will be set within three months, and thereafter every six months for as long as the child remains on the register.

Social work interventions

Ongoing direct work with the child (or by a specialist if required) and with the family will be undertaken to complete the assessment. Management of the case on a day-to-day basis will also involve collecting and analysing reports from specialists etc. and preparing reports for the core group meetings, conference review and court hearings (if relevant). If the child is being 'Looked After' supervised contact sessions with parents/family members will need to be arranged and managed. The key worker will also liaise with core group members, convening, attending and recording core group meetings. The social worker is required to prepare detailed and accurate reports for all stages of the child protection process and their involvement with the child could be on a long-term basis.

Family group conferences (FGCs)

FGCs are a positive option for working with, and planning services for the child and their family. FGCs enable everyone participating to find solutions to difficulties, which they and a child are facing. FGCs methodology has a good record of success in safeguarding children and enhancing the power of the family network, by removing the often bureaucratic mechanisms around child protection procedures. FGCs provide the space for practitioners to reflect upon and address their values, whilst also providing an opportunity for 'mothers' to tell their own stories about their situation and context (Marsh and Crow, 1997).

It is important to note that concerns about children and families in the child protection area can emerge or diminish at any time. The focus, whatever the circumstances are, must remain on the child and their welfare, by paying attention to the child's development, attachment relationships and the child's own wishes and feelings. Working with families where there are child protection concerns therefore demands highly competent practitioners who can manage complex issues, who actively keep themselves informed of legislation, policy and practice guidance and can maintain helpful relationships with adults and children as individuals (DoH, 1995; Bell and Watson, 2003).

Conclusion

Arguably social work with children and their families will be viewed more positively when we acknowledge and learn from the routinely 'good' practice that is undertaken through the thousands of interventions made each year by social workers. We should be able to celebrate this effective, demanding, often harrowing area of social work practice and commend those practitioners who continue to deliver this service every day, year in year out (Ferguson, 2005).

> *I believe that every-day social workers and other professionals, help many children to escape from intolerable abuse and neglect, and many families to steer themselves into happier, less self-destructive paths'*

(Beckett, 2007, p212)

FURTHER READING

Horwath, J (2007) *Child neglect: Identification and assessment.* Palgrave Macmillan
This book clarifies the issues and processes involved in identifying and assessing neglect and particularly explores the impact that neglect has upon the child's development and attachment strategies.

O'Hagan, K (2006) *Identifying emotional and psychological abuse.* Open University Press.
This book is particularly useful in providing case studies and vignettes to highlight normal development and abusive situations.

Cleaver, H, Unell, I, and Aldgate, J (1999) *Children's needs – parenting capacity: The impact of parental mental illness, problem alcohol and drug use and domestic violence on children's development.* The Stationery Office.
A useful text looking at issues which may impact on parenting.

Corby, B (2006) *Child abuse: towards a knowledge base,* 3rd edition. Buckingham: Open University Press.
This book provides a broad knowledge base for practitioners and students in all aspects of child protection.

Daniel, B, Wassell, S and Gilligan, R (1999) *Child development for child care and protection workers.* London: Jessica Kingsley.
A helpful text which relates child development and child protection, particularly for attachment theory.

Department of Health, NSPCC and The University of Sheffield (2001) *The child's world.* London: Jessica Kingsley.
This book focuses on assessment practice and achieving better outcomes for children and usefully discusses all aspects from the Framework for Assessment including children's developmental needs and parenting capacity

Chapter 5

Social Work with Children with Disabilities and their Families

Jackie Hughes

A C H I E V I N G   A   S O C I A L   W O R K   D E G R E E

This chapter will help you begin to meet the following National Occupational Standards:

Key Role 1: Prepare for and work with individuals, families, carers, groups and communities to assess their needs and circumstances.

- Prepare for social work contact and involvement.
- Work with individuals, families, carers, groups and communities to help them make informed decisions.
- Assess needs and options to recommend the course of action.

Key Role 2: Plan, carry out and review social work practice, with individuals, families, carers, groups, communities and other professionals.

- Interact with individuals, families, carers, groups, communities and professional colleagues.

Key Role 5: Manage and be accountable with supervision and support for your own social work practice within your own organisation.

- Manage and be accountable for your own work.

Key Role 6: Demonstrate professional competence in social work practice.

- Work within agreed standards of social work practice and ensure your own professional development.

It will also introduce you to the following academic standards as set out in the social work subject benchmark statement:

3.1.1. Social work services and service users.

- The social processes (associated with, for example, poverty, unemployment, poor health, disablement, lack of education and other sources of disadvantage) that lead to marginalisation, isolation and exclusion and their impact on the demand for social work services.
- The nature and validity of different definitions of, and explanations for, the characteristics and circumstances of service users and the services required by them.

3.1.4. Social work theory.

The subject skills highlighted to demonstrate this knowledge in practice include:

- Research-based concepts and critical explanations from social work theory and other disciplines that contribute to the knowledge base of social work, including their distinctive epistemological status and application to practice.
- The relevance of psychological and physiological perspectives to understanding individual and social development and functioning.

3.1.5 The nature of social work practice.
- The nature and characteristics of skills associated with effective practice, both direct and indirect, with a range of service users and in a variety of settings including group care.

3.2.2 Problem solving skills.
- 3.2.2.2 Gathering information.
- 3.2.2.3 Analysis and synthesis.
- 3.2.2.4 Intervention and evaluation.

5.2.1 Knowledge and understanding.
- Ability to use this knowledge and understanding in work within specific practice contexts.

Introduction

In this chapter you will consider some of the issues facing disabled children and their families so that you can develop your understanding, knowledge and skills to enable you to work effectively to support disabled children within their communities (Children Act 1989, section 17).

Different models of disability will be explored and an understanding of the social model will be used to help you promote inclusive social work practice. The views of disabled children and their families, and disabled adults, will be shown to be central to understanding some of the barriers to inclusion that disabled children face in their daily lives. The chapter will be based on *The Children Act 1989 Guidance and Regulations Volume 6 Children with Disabilities, Children Act 2004,* and the *National Service Framework Standard 8 for disabled children and young people and those with complex health needs.*

The first part of the chapter will focus on the different models of disability and an explanation of the social model of disability before considering some of the definitions of disability and terminology which you will encounter as a social work student. The views of disabled people about the use of language and acceptable terminology will be considered.

There will be an opportunity for you to think about some of the issues associated with prenatal testing and diagnosis of disability. Case examples will help you apply your knowledge to developing skills in communication with disabled children and their families.

Assessment will be considered in relation to the *Together from the Start* guidance (DoH, 2003, www.rightfromthestart.org.uk and www.essp.org.uk) and *Early Support Professional Guidance* (DoH/DFES, 2004, as previous websites), and multi-agency working and the importance for families of effective key working services will be explored (CCNUK Key working standards). Holistic assessments which include housing, as well as education and supports such as short-breaks, will be considered (DoH leisure/DFEE/Home Office, 2000). There will be an exploration of the vulnerability of disabled children (who are more likely to be abused than non-disabled children) and how to work to safeguard disabled children from abuse. Transition to adulthood is an important time for disabled young people and their families; the focus will be on the need to plan with disabled teenagers, their families and communities to ensure that our disabled young people develop valued opportunities as adults in education, employment, housing, leisure and relationships (*Aiming High for Disabled Children: Better Support for Families,* 2007).

Models of disability

There are different models explaining disability which have changed over time and in different societies as attitudes to disability have changed. Models of disability are influenced by the wider views in society, so the importance of religious explanations, which were once central, has declined in our increasingly secular society. The two main models of disability are the individual model (medical model) and the social model. When working with disabled children, it is important that a child is seen as a child first rather than a disabled child whatever your preferred model of disability. This does not mean that disabled children do not have particular health needs associated with their impairment that must also be met.

> *Ensuring equality of opportunity does not mean that all children are treated the same. It does mean understanding and working sensitively and knowledgeably with diversity.*
> (DoH/DfEE/Home Office, 2000, paragraph 1.4)

It is important to listen to the views of disabled children about what is important to them.

Young people say they want to:

- Be listened to when decisions are made about their lives.

- Have friends of the same age or who share similar experiences.

- Do the same things as other children and young people of their age – shopping, going to a cinema, clubbing, going to youth and sport clubs, playing football, etc.

- Have the opportunity to be involved in out-of-school activities.

- Be safe from harassment and bullying.

- Have control of spending money, and have enough money to enjoy life.

- Live in a society where they don't face prejudice.

(NSF for Children Standard 8, 2004 p8)

Medical model

The medical model is part of the individual model of disability, which locates the disability within the person, concentrating on the impairment. This view of disability tends to portray the disabled person as tragic or someone who is superhuman and has overcome obstacles (Oliver, 1983). The focus is on the impairment and prevention and cure, or rehabilitation and care. It may lead to provision of adaptations to enable the disabled person to 'fit in' to society with individual impairments seen as the cause of people's difficulties in functioning, rather than addressing the barriers to inclusion that disabled people face.

EXERCISE **5.1**

Can you think of examples of the medical model and how the focus on the individual and 'cure or care' might have influenced services for disabled children?

Comment

You may have thought about disabled children who have been provided with artificial limbs to make them seem non-disabled, or children who are wheelchair users spending long periods of time in physiotherapy during school time at the expense of their academic work. You may want to keep some notes to help you think about different ways in which disabled children are seen within the medical model. It is also important to recognise that disabled children may not have equality of access to medical care such as a community dentist or primary health care (Russell, 1995).

Social model

The social model was developed by disabled people who identified the barriers to their inclusion in a society which discriminates against disabled people (Oliver, 1990; Swain, et al., 1993). Disabled children are marginalised and segregated from society in leisure, education and opportunities that non-disabled children take for granted (Marchant, 2001). Historically, disabled children have been educated in segregated 'special' schools and separated from their peers in their communities.

EXERCISE **5.2**

Think about a disabled child you know. In what ways is the life of this child different from that of non-disabled children?

Comment

You may find that you had difficulty thinking of a disabled child because of the way that disabled children are marginalised in our society. Did you identify barriers to inclusion in terms of accessible play facilities, separate education or resourced provision/units in mainstream schools, accessible transport facilities?

You may also have identified the way that attitudes to disability may cause barriers to inclusion. Disabled children may not be invited to play at friends' houses or participate in the activities that non-disabled children take for granted.

Social-psychological model

The social-psychological model of disability highlights the importance of the experience of the disabled person, emphasises that disabled people should be listened to and recognises the way that some experiences of oppression may be internalised in ways that are not conscious (Marks, 1999a). Research with disabled children has identified that they see disability as only one aspect of their identity and in some situations other aspects may be more important: e.g. gender, ethnicity (Watson, et al., 1999).

Definitions of disability

Definitions of disability have changed over time according to different views of disability, and this is reflected in the language in different pieces of legislation. You will find that the definitions you encounter will vary, some may seem out-dated, particularly in older legislation such as the Chronically Sick and Disabled Person's Act. It is important to be aware of the power of language and the views of disabled people themselves (Barnes, 1992). Some people prefer the term *disabled* person because it identifies the way that people are disabled by society. Other people prefer *person with disabilities*, as it concentrates on the person first. People with learning disabilities often say they prefer the term *learning difficulties* (People First, London and Thames), although this has sometimes led to confusion with the term *specific learning difficulties* which is used in the Education Act 1981 to refer to dyslexia. The government uses the term *learning disabilities* in the *Valuing People White Paper* (2001). People First say *Label Jars not People*. I shall use the terms *disabled children* or *children with disabilities* within this chapter. We need to recognise the importance of language and the fact that this is developing. We need to listen to, and take account of, the views of disabled people themselves. It is important that we see disabled children as children first and develop services to ensure that they have the same rights as non-disabled children.

EXERCISE 5.3

Think about some of the ways that disabled children are portrayed in the media. How might that influence your perception of the abilities of disabled children?

N.B. You may want to collect magazine and newspaper articles and make notes about television or radio programmes that you have listened to or watched.

Comment

Did you find that disabled children are rarely portrayed in the media? If they are it may be a token disabled child, rather than a central character in the programme. Were disabled children portrayed positively, or did you find that the disabled children were seen as evoking pity? You may also want to look at children's books and consider how disabled children feature in books or whether they are largely absent. How might this affect the self-esteem of disabled children?

Diagnosis

Research summary

The Family Resources Survey 2002-3 estimates that there are approximately 700,000 disabled children under 16 in Great Britain. There is an increased incidence of children with severe and complex disabilities as well as increasing numbers of children who are being diagnosed with autistic spectrum disorders. The reasons for this are due to a number of factors including: improved medical care leading to the survival of more pre-term babies and children who have experienced severe trauma and illness. In addition, children with complex disabilities are surviving and living longer with improved medical treatment and the availability of assistive technology. The NSF for Children, Young People and Maternity Services recognises that the majority of disabled children live with their families. Marchant (2001) points out that everyone working with children should be working with disabled children sometimes as 3–5 per cent of children are disabled (DoH, 1998a; OPCS, 1986). There are more disabled children in social class V than in social class I, and there is a link between disability and poverty in household income. The cost of bringing up a child with a disability is approximately three times the cost for a non-disabled child (Baldwin, 1985; Dobson and Middleton, 1998).

Right from the Start is guidance based on a template developed by Scope working with parents of disabled children, disabled people and voluntary organisations. It is a framework for professionals to develop good practice in communicating with parents about diagnosis of disability. The Good Practice Framework covers all areas to do with the communication of the diagnosis, including who should be present and next steps in term of practical help and information (www.rightfromthestart.org.uk).

EXERCISE 5.4

You are asked to be present at a discussion with parents, which will inform them of the diagnosis of a disability for their child. What things might be important for you, as a professional, to consider in preparing for this meeting?

Comment

You might have recognised that many children do not receive a diagnosis as a young baby in hospital, but parents may become concerned that their child is not developing in the way that they had expected. Parents say that what is important to them is that their child is seen as important. 'Valuing the child' can be done by: showing respect for the child, using the child's name, talking positively about the child and avoiding making predictions, keep the baby or the child with the parents wherever possible to share the diagnosis. Respect for parents and families is also important and developing partnership with parents at this stage is crucial for positive relationships to develop with professionals who may continue to be involved in their child's life.

Perl Kingsley describes the experience of diagnosis of disability as similar to a journey: where parents have planned a trip to Italy but find themselves touching down in Holland instead. Their plans had included visits to the Coliseum, Michelangelo's *David* and the gondolas in Venice. It was not what they had planned when they set out on their journey, but as they look around they find that Holland has windmills and tulips and Rembrandts, too. The trip is different to what they had expected but just as beautiful. (Printed in DIAL–Disablement Information and Advice Line.)

Randall and Parker (1999) also deal with this complex and emotionally sensitive search for a diagnosis.

Right from the Start template

Key principles

Valuing the child

- *All children are unique – it is vital that professionals see the child first and and their condition/disability second.*
- *The child's name should be used at all times.*
- *Keep discussion about the child positive and avoid making predictions.*
- *Whenever possible keep the baby or the child with the parents when sharing the findings and diagnosis.*
- *If it is not appropriate for the baby or child to be present, remember to communicate in a way that shows respect for the child.*

Respect parents and families

- *Support and empower parents.*
- *Treat all parents' concerns seriously.*
- *Listen to parents and share information sensitively and honestly.*
- *Use plain and understandable language and give explanations to build parents' confidence.*
- *Acknowledge and respect cultural difference.*
- *Give opportunities to ask questions and check parents' understanding of the situation.*
- *Avoid giving negative non-verbal messages before concerns have been shared with parents.*

Right from the Start Template www.rightfromthestart.org.uk

Assessment

> *Children and young people who are disabled or who have complex health needs receive co-ordinated, high-quality child and family-centred services which are based on assessed needs, which promote social inclusion and, where possible, which enable them and their families to live ordinary lives.*
>
> (NSF for Children Standard 8, 2004 p5)

The Early Support Programme (www.espp.org.uk) is putting into practice the principles outlined in the government guidance document *Together From the Start*, which was published in May 2003. Right from the Start identified the way that families with disabled children may experience numerous assessments by different professionals, adding to the stress that families may already be experiencing. The *Early Support Programme Professional Guidance* states that:

Effective, joint multi-agency assessment in the early years means:
- *Co-ordinating action, particularly where different aspects of a child's situation need to be assessed by different people.*
- *Responding to a family's need to get reliable information as quickly as possible and learn from more than one perspective at a time.*
- *Ensuring that initial assessment leads to action and prompt provision of information and practical help.*

(2004, p44)

Disabled children have a right to assessments as 'children in need' under section 17 of the Children Act 1989. The Green Paper *Every Child Matters* (Chief Secretary to the Treasury) indicates that there needs to be a common assessment framework. Social workers need, at present, to follow the guidance in the *Framework for the Assessment of Children in Need and their Families*, 2000. This includes the child's development, the family's needs and capacities, as well as environmental factors such as housing. The initial and/or core assessments can be used as the basis for the development of the *Family Service Plan*, agreed by the family and agencies working with them (see Chapter 3).

In addition, the assessment should take into account the needs of parent carers.

The assessment of a disabled child must address the needs of the parent carers. Recognising the needs of parent carers is a core component in agreeing services which will promote the welfare of the disabled child.
(Assessing Children in Need and their Families: Practice Guidance Section 3.6 DoH, 2000)

CASE STUDY

Will Adams is a 2-year-old child who was born with a rare syndrome, resulting in complex disabilities including dual sensory loss (hearing and visual impairment) and congenital heart problems which meant that Will had several operations at a very young age. His mother gave up employment to become a full-time carer to Will. Her health visitor has asked social services to complete an assessment for Will and his family as she is concerned that Will's mother is physically and emotionally exhausted.

(By permission of Kirklees Parent Carer Forum)

EXERCISE 5.5

As the social worker responsible for undertaking an assessment for Will and his family, in your opinion:

- *What are the issues?*

- *Who else might you involve in the assessment?*

- *What plans might you consider?*

Comment

You will have recognised that Will requires a holistic assessment that takes into account a range of issues which include his health needs, housing and leisure activities, as well as education and social services' support. You may also have thought about the different professionals that may be involved with Will and his family. These could include: GP, health visitor, paediatrician, speech therapist, portage worker, physiotherapist, and occupational therapist. Will may attend tertiary health care centres because of the complexity of his health needs, resulting in numerous appointments and assessments. You may have suggested that Will and his family should have a key worker to facilitate the maze of services involved with them. You may also wish to undertake a carer's assessment for Will's mum under the Carers and Disabled Children Act (2001) and Carers (Equal Opportunities) Act 2004, to identify what supports she may need in her caring role.

Communication

> *Nothing about us without us.*

This quotation from the disabled people's movement is an important reminder of the need to ensure participation for disabled children. Disabled people have argued for inclusion, not only in society as a whole, but in fundamental decisions about their lives. Non-disabled children have frequently found themselves excluded from important decisions in their lives, but disabled children may still be routinely excluded from important meetings such as education or social services reviews. Disabled children give examples of ways in which they have been excluded by not having their views sought (Marchant, 2001; Morris, 1998b). Social workers and other professionals working with disabled children need to ensure that they routinely involve children in the assessment and decision-making process.

EXERCISE **5.6**

You have been asked to work with a child who has a learning disability or a communication impairment. What would you do to find out their wishes?

Comment

Good communication skills are important in communicating with all children, not just disabled children. You may have thought about being child-centred and taking the child's age and interests into account. Children may be more relaxed in environments that are familiar to them. Good listening skills, being prepared to take extra time or use play skills are all important. Do not be frightened to ask a child to repeat themselves if you have not understood. If a child does not use verbal communication you will need to ensure that you observe carefully their non-verbal communication, which may include gestures, facial expression, body language or behaviour. Use a carer, friend, or someone who knows the child well to help if you are uncertain of their communication. Some children may use alternative methods of communication which may include BSL (British Sign Language) or Makaton (a form of sign language used to augment verbal communication) or symbols.

All children can communicate: we need to be aware of the barriers which affect their participation.

Key working

> *My child isn't split into three pieces.*
>
> (National Service Framework Standard 8: Key worker standards CCNUK)

Parents of disabled children have identified the benefits for them of having a key worker to assist them to deal with the complex network of services with which they are involved. As children grow and develop their needs change and so the process of assessments and reviews may be ongoing, involving education and housing as well as health and social services. Parents who have had the benefit of a key worker report satisfaction with the support that they receive through having a named worker who is able to help them co-ordinate services.

> *A key worker or lead professional is both a source of support for the families of disabled children and a link by which other services are accessed and used effectively. They have responsibility for working together with the family and with professionals from their own and other services and for ensuring delivery of the plan for the child and family. Workers performing this role may come from a number of different agencies, depending on the particular needs of the child.*
>
> (Together from the Start, p87 (www.espp.org.uk))

Safeguarding disabled children

Children with disabilities have the same rights to protection as all children, but research indicates that disabled children are more vulnerable to abuse than non-disabled children (Westcott and Cross, 1996), and yet they are less likely to be represented in the child protection system (Morris,1995, 1998a, 1999).

EXERCISE 5.7

Consider some of the reasons that disabled children may be particularly vulnerable to abuse.

Comment

You may have identified the way that disabled children are marginalised in society and tend to be more isolated from their communities. You may also have considered some of the ways in which services are provided to disabled children and their families, leading to disabled children being cared for by more adults than non-disabled children in residential or 'special' schools away from their families. You may also have thought about the need for personal assistance, which may increase the vulnerability of disabled children to abuse.

RESEARCH SUMMARY

There are important issues to consider in relation to the vulnerability of disabled children to abuse:

- *Social attitudes towards disability;*

- *Special treatment of disabled children;*

- *Denial of sexuality for disabled people.*

(Marchant, 2001)

Social attitudes toward disability have led to the attitude that as disabled children are 'tragic' nobody would abuse a disabled child. Paradoxically, the alternative stereotype that a disabled child is not 'perfect' has led to assumptions that abuse may matter less (Westcott and Cross, 1996). The way that disabled children are marginalised in society may increase their vulnerability to abuse: they may be more isolated, be more dependent and have less control over their lives (Marchant, 2001). The way that support services are provided to disabled children and their families may also increase their vulnerability, with more adults caring for them than non-disabled children and periods of time spent in respite or residential settings, without the usual safeguards for children living away from their families (Morris, 1995). Research has indicated that disabled children in residential education or respite placements may not be treated as 'looked after' children and not be afforded the safeguards of the Children Act (Russell, 1995; Platts et al., 1996). The denial of the sexuality of disabled people may lead to a lack of sex education for disabled children, increasing their vulnerability (Marchant, 2001).

Leisure

Disabled children may not experience the same leisure opportunities as non-disabled children because of barriers to participation. Parents from the Kirklees Parent Carer Forum (workshop with social work students, University of Leeds, 2005) explained that it is difficult for their children to participate in activities that many non-disabled children take for granted. Playgrounds may not be accessible for children with mobility impairments, a child with a hearing impairment may need a communicator, or lack of accessible transport may mean that a parent has to take a child to leisure activities. Some parents explain that their children are simply not invited to friends' houses to play, because of distance from friends' homes where children attend special schools, inaccessible houses, or lack of personal assistants to enable them to participate (Marchant, 2001).

The Disability Discrimination Act 1995 includes leisure activities in its remit. These examples from parents highlight the importance of inclusion for disabled children and emphasise that leisure opportunities don't just happen for disabled children in the way that they do for non-disabled children; disabled children may be excluded from society by acts of omission as well as commission. This also applies to services, which may act as if disabled children are invisible.

Short breaks

Social services have a duty to publicise services for disabled children, but many families describe accessing services as a 'battle' to get the supports that they need for their disabled children. Christine Lenehan, Director of the Council for Disabled Children (2004), identifies the way that parents may become *warring parents* as they struggle to access services. The challenge to services is to develop services which value the child and work in partnership with parents as children's needs change. Of particular concern is the need to ensure that services are accessible to families where there is more than one child with a disability and to families from ethnic communities (Shah, 1995).

Traditionally, services have offered respite to families with disabled children. The use of the term respite suggests that disabled children are a burden and the service is for families, rather than the child. A study of the needs of children with learning disabilities and complex health needs (Platts, et al., 1996) found that for parents to benefit from a short break they needed to know that their children were happy. Parents valued the opportunity to have a flexible service which included babysitting, day time activities, care in the family home or overnight stays. Families from ethnic communities appreciated flexible short breaks with families who knew their children well. One Asian parent commented that she would be unable to go out in the holidays with her children without the short-break carer as she had two children who used wheel-chairs. She particularly valued this support within the home, which enabled them to do the things that many families take for granted. Short breaks are valued by families but should also be child-centred for the child, parents and other siblings to benefit. One parent at a parent workshop (Russell, 1995) commented that her child was *no longer a shadow in someone else's* eyes when her child was able to have short breaks with another family.

The importance of short breaks for families and for their children was recognised in the disabled children's review by the government. Aiming High for Disabled Children: Better Support for Families included a specific grant of £280 million for short breaks for the period 2008-2011.

Housing

Housing is an area which needs to be included in assessments. Oldman and Beresford (2002) identified the importance of housing for disabled children and their families. Nine out of ten families who were interviewed for their research reported at least one housing need, with many reporting multiple needs. Many families described the difficulties of space for their children. This was not just space for children with mobility difficulties to move around in their wheel-chairs, but included space for equipment, adequate space for children with challenging behaviours or sleep problems and for their brothers and sisters. Disabled children want to be able to use the kitchen and communal areas of the family home as well as accessing the garden. Many families report lack of adaptations and delays in the provision of equipment exacerbating the strains of caring for disabled children. Although there is some financial support available the limitations of the Disabled Facilities Grant may mean that families are unable to afford the necessary adaptations, particularly for children with profound and complex needs. (Beresford 2006)

Education

Historically disabled children have been educated in segregated special schools. Under the 1944 Education Act, children with learning disabilities were described as ineducable. It was not until 1971 that children with learning disabilities became entitled to education, but this was in special schools according to the diagnosis of disability. The 1978 Warnock Committee advocated the integration of disabled children into mainstream schools and integration was promoted under the 1981 Education Act. The proviso was that this should be in accordance with the efficient use of resources and as long as it did not affect the education of other pupils. However, one of the benefits of inclusive education is the opportunity for non-disabled children to learn from their disabled peers. The 1996 Education Act continued the policy of integration but many disabled children continue to be educated in special schools rather than included in their local community schools. Not all disabled children will have special educational needs, but for many children they will have a formal assessment process led by education where the LEA is considering a Statement of Special Educational Needs (Special Educational Needs and Disability Act, 2001). Social workers will be expected to contribute reports as part of the assessment process.

Some children may be educated at residential special schools and these children should be regarded as looked after children with the protection and safeguards of the 1989 Children Act. The supervision provided by social services varies between local authorities, and Morris (1998a) found that many children were not consulted. The White Paper, Care Matters: Time for Change 2007, recognised the importance of consultation and involvement of disabled young people, and discussed the Looked after Children status for disabled children.

Transition

Children with a Statement of Special Educational Needs should have an Annual Review. The Review following a disabled child's 14th birthday is known as the Transition Review as plans should start being formulated with them for their future. At each subsequent Review, the Transition Plan should be considered and amendments made if necessary. This should be the basis for future planning and should include areas such as social services support, housing, as well as education. The *Valuing People* White Paper 2001 for people with learning disabilities prioritised transition as a time for Person Centred Planning. Person Centred Plans focus on the person who is being planned with, their friends and family, identifying core components for Essential Life Style Plans and PATHS (Planning Alternative Tomorrows with Hope) (O'Brien, 2002). Morris (1999) describes the experiences of disabled young people at transition as *Hurtling into the Void*, her research recommends good practice guidelines for services working with disabled young people to promote positive futures. The difficulties faced by disabled young people at transition was recognised in the government review of services for disabled children, and Aiming High for Disabled Children included £19 million for a Transition Support Programme modelled on the Early Support Programme.

If we are really going to develop an inclusive society which values people, then creative assessments, working in partnership with disabled young people and their families, must work towards achieving 'alternative tomorrows' today.

FURTHER READING

Marchant, R (2001) Working with disabled children. In Foley, et al., (eds) (2001) *Children in society: Contemporary theory, policy and practice*. Basingstoke: Palgrave.
This chapter gives a useful overview of a range of issues for social workers working with children with disabilities.

Morris, J (1999) *Hurtling into the void: Transition to adulthood for young people with 'complex health and support needs'*. Brighton: JRF Pavilion.
This book will be helpful to all students working with disabled young people at transition.

Shah, R (1995) *The silent minority. Children with disabilities in Asian families*. Derby: National Children's Bureau.
This book helps social work students recognise the oppression faced by disabled children and their families from Black and minority ethnic families.

Westcott, H and Cross, M (1996) *This far and no further: Towards ending the abuse of disabled children*. Birmingham: Venture Press.
This is particularly relevant for all professionals working with disabled children to enable them to work towards safeguarding children from abuse.

Useful contacts
Contact a Family: 170 Tottenham Court Road, London W1 0HA
Council for Disabled Children: 8 Wakley St, London EC1V 7QE

Resources and professional guidance
Department of Health (2000) *Assessing children in need and their families: Practice guidance*.
Chapter 3: Assessing the needs of disabled children and their families.

Department for Education and Employment (2001) *SEN Code of Practice*.

Contact a Family (2004) *Working with families affected by a disability or health condition from pregnancy to pre-school*.

Parent participation: improving services for disabled children.

Contact a Family and Council for Disabled Children (2004) Professionals Guide.

WEBSITES

www.ccnuk.org.uk
www.contactafamily.co.uk
www.councilfordisabledchildren.co.uk
www.dfes.org.uk
www.doh.org.uk
www.espp.org.uk
www.jrf.co.uk
www.rightfromthestart.org.uk
www.sharedcarenetwork.co.uk

Chapter 6

Substitute Care for Children

Maureen O' Loughlin and Steve O' Loughlin

A C H I E V I N G   A   S O C I A L   W O R K   D E G R E E

This chapter will focus on the three main areas of substitute care (agency fostering, adoption and residential care). It will help you to meet the following National Occupational Standards:

Key Role 1: Prepare for and work with individuals, families, carers, groups, and communities to assess their needs and circumstances.
- Prepare for social work contact and involvement.
- Work with individuals, families, carers, groups and communities to help them make informed decisions.
- Assess needs and options to recommend a course of action.

Key Role 2: Plan, carry out, review and evaluate social work practice with individuals, families, carers, communities and other professionals.
- Work with individuals, families, carers, groups and communities to identify, gather, analyse and understand information.
- Prepare, produce, implement and evaluate plans with individuals, families, carers, groups, communities and professional colleagues.

Key Role 5: Manage and be accountable with supervision and support for your own social work practice within your organisation.
- Regularly monitor, review and evaluate changes in needs and circumstances.

Key Role 6: Demonstrate professional competence in social work practice.
- Review and update your own knowledge of legal, policy and procedural frameworks.

It will also introduce you to the following academic standards set out in the social work subject benchmark statement:

3.1.1 Social work service and service users.
- The social processes (associated with, for example, poverty, unemployment, poor health, disablement, lack of education and other sources of disadvantage) that lead to marginalisation, isolation and exclusion and their impact on the demand for social work services.

3.2.2 Problem solving skills.
- Gathering information.
- Analysis and synthesis.
- Intervention and evaluation.

Introduction

Substitute care is provided by local authorities, voluntary, private and independent agencies. These agencies provide accommodation for children in a number of different ways. This chapter will introduce and discuss the different types of substitute care which are available to children including:

- fostering

- adoption

- residential care.

Children are cared for in the Looked After Children System (LAC) in different ways and for different reasons, which include:

- **Short breaks** Children being cared for as part of a package of support, for example a child with disabilities (Children Act 1989, sections 17 and 20).

- **Accommodation** Children being cared for as part of an agreement with parents or those with parental responsibility, or if a child has been abandoned or there is no one who has parental responsibility for them (Children Act 1989, section 20).

- **Care and related orders** Children who are the subject of care or interim care orders; freeing for adoption orders or emergency protection or police protection orders.

- **Offending** Children and young people on remand or subject to some orders made by the youth court.

An analysis of children looked after at 31 March between the years 2003 and 2007 is shown in Table 6.1. The table shows the ages, gender, category of need and ethnic origin of children and young people for these years. The statistics show that there are more males in the system than females and that there are peaks in ages (10 to 15), which is worth reflecting on in terms of the life course and your knowledge of child development. What factors do you think might cause this peak? (See Chapter 5 in *Social Work and Human Development*, Crawford and Walker, 2007 for further discussion.) As you will see although the table gives information about children's ages and gender there is now information about ethnicity and category of need as well as disability. The percentage of children and young people who started to be looked after in the year ending 31st March 2007 who were white British has decreased over the last 5 years from 77 per cent in 2003 to 74 per cent in 2007 indicating a rise in the numbers of Black and ethnic minority children within the system.

Comment

Age and gender clearly impact on the relative numbers of children and young people in the LAC system. However research has shown that Black and minority ethnic children are increasingly over-represented whilst there is little information with regard to the experience of children with disabilities in the LAC system (Barn, 1993; Ince, 1998; Morris, 1998; Kirton, 2000; Flynn, 2002). These statistics are useful for providing a basis for planning appropriate provision, and considering developing trends in the LAC system.

Table 6.1 *Children looked after at 31 March by gender, age at 31 March, category of need, and ethnic origin, 2003–2007*[1,2,3]

England   rates per 0,000 children under 18 years

	2003[4]	2004[5]	2005[5]	2006[5]	2007[5]
All children looked after[1] at 31 March[1,2]	61,200	61,200	61,000	60,300	60,000
Rates per 10,000 children under 18 years	55	55	55	55	55

numbers and percentages

	numbers					percentages				
	2003[4]	2004[5]	2005[5]	2006[5]	2007[5]	2003[4]	2004[5]	2005[5]	2006[5]	2007[5]
All children looked after at 31 March[1,2]	61,200	61,200	61,000	60,300	60,000	100	100	100	100	100
Gender	61,200	61,200	61,000	60,300	60,000	100	100	100	100	100
Male	33,800	33,900	33,700	33,400	33,400	55	55	55	55	56
Female	27,400	27,200	27,200	27,900	26,600	45	45	45	45	44
Age at 31 March (years)	61,200	61,200	61,000	60,300	60,000	100	100	100	100	100
Under 1	2,700	2,700	2,800	2,900	3,000	4	4	5	5	5
1 to 4	9,100	8,900	8,600	8,400	8,800	15	15	14	14	15
5 to 9	13,300	12,700	12,100	11,500	10,900	22	21	20	19	18
10 to 15	26,700	26,600	26,600	26,200	25,500	44	43	44	43	42
16 and over	9,500	10,400	10,800	11,300	11,800	16	17	18	19	20
Category of need[6]	61,200	61,200	61,000	60,300	60,000	100	100	100	100	100
Abuse or neglect	38,800	38,200	38,200	37,600	37,200	63	62	63	62	62
Child's disability	2,500	2,400	2,400	2,400	2,300	4	4	4	4	4
Parents illness or disability	3,500	3,400	3,300	3,200	3,000	6	6	5	5	5
Family in acute distress	4,200	4,200	4,400	4,500	4,800	7	7	7	7	8
Family dysfunction	6,100	6,100	6,100	6,100	6,400	10	10	10	10	11
Socially unacceptable behaviour	1,800	1,700	1,500	1,300	1,300	3	3	2	2	2
Low income	90	110	110	110	120	0	0	0	0	0
Absent parenting	4,200	4,900	5,000	5,100	5,000	7	8	8	8	8
Ethnic origin	61,200	61,200	61,000	60,300	60,000	100	100	100	100	100
White										
White British	47,300	46,300	45,900	45,000	44,700	77	76	75	75	74
White Irish	580	520	500	440	400	1	1	1	1	1
Any other White Background	1,800	1,900	1,800	1,600	1,500	3	3	3	3	3
Mixed										
White and Black Caribbean	2,000	2,000	2,000	1,900	1,900	3	3	3	3	3
White and Black African	400	410	440	430	440	1	1	1	1	1
White and Asian	750	720	720	750	770	1	1	1	1	1
Any other mixed background	2,000	2,000	2,000	2,000	2,000	3	3	3	3	3
Asian or Asian British										
Indian	300	300	280	300	290	0	0	0	0	0
Pakistani	510	520	580	610	660	1	1	1	1	1
Bangladeshi	200	230	270	280	280	0	0	0	0	0
Any other Asian background	320	460	650	880	1,000	1	1	1	1	2

Table 6.1 (continued)

	2003[4]	2004[5]	2005[5]	2006[5]	2007[5]	2003[4]	2004[5]	2005[5]	2006[5]	2007[5]
Black or Black British										
Caribbean	1,600	1,700	1,600	1,600	1,600	3	3	3	3	3
African	1,800	2,300	2,400	2,400	2,300	3	4	4	4	4
Any other Black background	870	880	900	900	880	1	1	1	1	1
Other ethnic groups										
Chinese	80	120	120	120	130	0	0	0	0	0
Any other ethnic group	750	840	900	1,000	1,200	1	1	1	2	0

1. Figures exclude children looked after under an agreed series of short-term placements
2. Figures are taken from the CLA100 return
3. Figures are taken from the SSDA903 return
4. Includes children who are on remand, committed for trial or detained, and children subject to emergency orders or police protection. Figures in 2000 include children who are subject to a compulsory order under Section 53 of 1933 CYPA
5. Includes secure units, homes and hostels but excludes residential schools
6. Includes residential schools, lodgings and other residential settings

Source: DfES (2004) Children looked after at 31 March 2000–2004. The Stationery Office.

Children who are looked after

No matter how a child enters the looked after system the local authority has responsibilities towards that child, these include a duty to safeguard and promote their welfare (Children Act, 1989 s22 (3)). This duty should encompass all areas of a child's life and underlines the importance of the responsibility of the corporate parent in ensuring that all a child's needs are met, for example: educational, religious, cultural.

> **CASE STUDY**
>
> *Kylie is placed in a residential children's home. She is going out at night and will not say where, she is reluctant to go to school nor is the home providing her with an appropriate diet or care for her hair and skin. Is the local authority fulfilling its duty as a corporate parent?*

Table 6.2 gives information on the types of placements experienced as well as types of court orders, age and gender. The table shows that some children who are the subject of full or interim care orders are living with parents but because of the orders they are still part of the looked after system.

The local authority should also try to find out what the wishes and feelings of the child, their parents or those with parental responsibility and anyone else who has a reasonable interest in the child, are so that these can be taken into account both in terms of day-to-day living and also in longer term planning. A person with *reasonable interest* in a child could be a relative (aunt, uncle, grandparent, etc.) or a non-relative (close family friend). The prime factors for consideration are their importance to the child and their level of involvement with them. When decisions are made about *reasonable interest* the amount of meaningful *contact* a person has had with the child will be of particular importance. The Children Act 1989 gives an expectation that *due regard* must be given to the child's wishes and feelings but this must take into account their age and level of understanding as well as their religion, race, culture and their language (Children Act 1989 s22 (4) and (5)). This can be an area of tension as social workers have an overriding duty to put the welfare of the child or young person first (Children Act 1989 s1).

Table 6.2 *Children looked after at 31 March by placement, 2003–2007*[1,2,3]

England   **numbers and percentages**

	numbers					percentages				
	2003[4]	2004[5]	2005[5]	2006[5]	2007[5]	2003[4]	2004[5]	2005[5]	2006[5]	2007[5]
All children looked after at 31 March[1,2]	61,200	61,200	61,000	60,300	60,000	100	100	100	100	100
Foster placements	41,000	41,200	41,300	41,700	42,300	67	67	68	69	71
Foster placement inside Council boundary										
With relative or friend	5,800	5,800	5,600	5,300	5,100	9	9	9	9	8
With other foster carer										
provided by Council	21,900	21,000	20,400	20,000	20,200	36	34	33	33	34
arranged through agency	1,100	1,400	1,600	2,000	2,400	2	2	3	3	4
Foster placement outside Council boundary										
With relative or friend	1,900	2,000	2,000	2,000	1,900	3	3	3	3	3
With other foster carer										
provided by Council	4,900	5,100	5,200	5,400	5,300	8	8	9	9	9
arranged through agency	5,300	6,100	6,500	7,000	7,400	9	10	11	12	12
Placed for adoption[6]	3,800	3,600	3,400	3,000	2,500	6	6	6	5	4
Placed for adoption with consent										
with current foster carer (under S19 AA 2002)					130					0
Placed for adoption with placement order			360	360				1	1	
with current foster carer (under S21 AA 2002)					150					0
Placed for adoption with consent not with current foser carer (under S19 AA 2002)	3,800	3,600			640	6	6			1
Placed for adoption with placement order			3,100	2,700				5	4	
not with current foster carer (under S21 AA 2002)					1,600					3
Placement with parents	6,300	5,900	5,800	5,400	5,100	10	10	9	9	9
Other placement in the community	1,300	1,500	1,500	1,600	1,600	2	2	3	3	3
Living independently	1,200	1,500	1,500	1,600	1,600	2	2	2	3	3
Residential employment	–	10	10	–	–	–	0	0	–	–
secure units, children's homes and hostels	6,800	7,000	7,000	6,600	6,500	11	11	11	11	11
Secure unit inside Council boundary	40	30	30	20	30	0	0	0	0	0
Secure unit outside Council boundary[7]	210	210	220	170	170	0	0	0	0	0
Homes and hostels subject to Children's Homes regulations										
inside Council boundary	3,300	3,200	3,000	3,000	2,900	5	5	5	5	5
outside Council boundary	2,700	2,600	2,600	2,300	2,300	4	4	4	4	4
Homes and hostels *not* subject to Children's Homes regulations	530	910	1,100	1,100	1,100	1	1	2	2	2

Table 6.2 (continued)

England	numbers					percentages				
	2003[4]	2004[5]	2005[5]	2006[5]	2007[5]	2003[4]	2004[5]	2005[5]	2006[5]	2007[5]
Other residential settings	600	560	560	570	570	610	1	1	1	1
Residential care homes	220	200	210	230	230	0	0	0	0	0
NHS Trust providing medical/ nursing care	90	80	90	80	70	0	0	0	0	0
Family centre or mother and baby unit	170	130	150	120	150	0	0	0	0	0
Young offenders institution or prison	110	140	110	140	160	0	0	0	0	0
Residential schools	1,300	1,200	1,100	1,100	1,100	2	2	2	2	2
Missing – Absent for more than 24 hours from agreed placement	120	120	140	140	160	0	0	0	0	0
In refuge (section 51 of Children Act, 1989)	–	0	0	–	–	–	0	0	–	–
Whereabouts known (not in refuge)	40	40	20	20	30	0	0	0	0	0
Whereabouts unknown	80	90	120	120	120	0	0	0	0	0
Other placement	100	110	100	120	120	0	0	0	0	0

1. Source: SSDA903 return on children looked after.
2. Figures exclude children looked after under an agreed series of short term placements.
3. Historical data may differ from older publications. This is mainly due to the implementation of amendments and corrections sent by some local authorities after the publication date of previous materials.
4. Figures are delivered from the SSDA903 one third sample survey.
5. Figures are taken from the SSDA903 return which, since 2003–04 has covered all children looked after.
6. Since 2004–05 placed for adoption has been disaggregated by whether the placement is or is not with current foster carer. In 2006–07 placement also disaggregated according to whether consent was given or a placement order sought.
7. There are currently only 19 secure units operating in England therefore most placements will inevitably be outside the council boundary.

ACTIVITY **6.1**

What do you think due regard *means? How do you think a child's age and understanding might affect this? Would the level of* due regard *be different for a child of 4, a young person of 12 and a 16-year-old with learning difficulties? What would influence your answer?*

Comment

The age and level of understanding of the child or young person are of particular relevance but in the context of their particular situation, for example if there are allegations of abuse or high levels of neglect which are impacting on health and well being. For example Kylie, who is aged 12 and has learning disabilities, wants to go home to live. Her stepfather is alleged to have sexually abused her. In these circumstances as a social worker what would you have to put first, Kylie's wishes or her welfare? If the same situation arose with Tariq who is 4 and has been physically injured in the care of his parents would your dilemma be easier to resolve?

Care planning

Once a child is being looked after the local authority has to make a care plan, in consultation with the child and their parents, which has to be reviewed on a regular basis. If a child is looked after for four months a plan to achieve a permanent placement has to be made (*Review of Children's Cases (Amendment) (England) Regulations 2004*). These regulations introduce the Independent Reviewing Officer who has a duty to monitor care plans and take an active problem-solving role on behalf of the child. As part of their role they will need to ensure that consideration is given to plans for permanence for the child at an early stage of being *looked after* to ensure that they are not allowed to remain in the system through lack of planning and drift.

They have a further duty to refer children's cases to the Children and Families Courts Advisory and Support Service (CAFCASS) for legal action on behalf of the child to be considered. This provision has been introduced to help address the issue of detrimental delay in decision making for children (Parker, 1999; Lowe and Murch, 1999). There are prescribed minimum intervals for reviews, although additional reviews can be convened in response to circumstances or on the request of a child or parent:

* within four weeks of a child becoming looked after;

* not more than three months after the first review;

* not more than six months after the previous review.

Before holding reviews the *responsible authority* (the local authority or the voluntary agency that is accommodating the child) must consult with, and seek the views of, a number of people including the child, their parent/s or anyone else with parental responsibility, foster carer, residential staff, health visitor, GP. All these people should be invited to the review, attending for as much of it as is thought appropriate, they will also be notified of the results of the review and any decisions taken (*Review of Children's Cases Regulations, 1991*).

Looked after children have to receive a health assessment, which may include a physical examination, at specified intervals (every six months for children under 5 and 12 months for those over 5). Children who are of sufficient age and understanding may refuse to co-operate with medical examinations. This may result in dilemmas and conflicts for the social worker which are not easily resolved (Fostering Services Regulations, 2002). Each responsible authority should have written procedures for reviews but these may not always help to resolve dilemmas. Venues are supposed to be chosen in consultation with children, parents and carers though this may not help if there is conflict between their views not only about place but also about who should attend. Social workers need to think about who will offer support to children and parents during the review as their needs and views may be very different.

The next activity will help you to begin to have an understanding of the dilemmas involved in the review process.

Kylie is attending her review with her social worker. Her stepfather has been invited, she does not want him there but her mother will not attend without him. Kylie is also due to have her annual health assessment, this time with a physical examination as she has been having frequent stomach pains. She has, however, refused to co-operate with this. What are the dilemmas in this situation for the social worker and the independent reviewing officer? How might they be resolved?

Comment

Kylie should be consulted about her review, as should her mother. This difference in views raises dilemmas, which may not be able to be resolved and may necessitate the review having to be split to enable everyone to attend. At the same time it also raises the dilemma of Kylie's wishes being overridden, possibly because she is a young person with learning difficulties.

You will need to think about Kylie's right to refuse an examination balanced against her interests if she has a medical problem that needs attention. There may be ways she would agree if she had some control over what was happening, for example some choice of examiner and possibly venue. Time would be needed to help her work through her anxieties to see if they could be resolved.

Fostering

This section will discuss and consider the different types of fostering available to children and the processes involved in the provision of foster care. Fostering, formerly called *boarding out*, has existed informally for many years. However it is only since the *Monckton Report*, 1945 and the *Curtis Report*, 1946, which were both concerned with the care of children living away from home, that the need for quality controls and supervision was recognised. The *Monckton Report* 1945 was particularly influential as it was an inquiry into the death of a child, Dennis O'Neill (a 13 year-old boy) who was starved and beaten to death by his foster father. The subsequent Children Act 1948 envisaged children living with ordinary families as opposed to living in residential care or with carers under informal arrangements which offered few safeguards for their welfare. Fostering has developed since that time.

This section will discuss and consider the different types of fostering currently available to children and the processes involved in the provision of foster care. Fostering services are provided by a variety of agencies including local authorities and voluntary (not for profit) organisations. Over recent years a growing number of independent agencies have developed, providing services through business agreements. Local authorities can make arrangements for its fostering services in respect of a child to be delegated to an independent fostering agency if that is the most effective way of achieving a placement for a child. This is happening more and more frequently as local authorities struggle to provide sufficient foster carers. These arrangements are regulated and should ensure that all independent agencies have a manager who is registered with the Commission for Social Care

Inspection. The manager must ensure that the welfare of children is safeguarded and promoted at all times (Fostering Services Regulations, 2002).

What is fostering?

In simple terms fostering relates to the care of children within a family environment by people who are not their parents or those with parental responsibility. This short definition hides a complex set of relationships which can be considered in five categories, although one survey found 47 different classifications among local authorities (Waterhouse, 1997).

The five categories are:

• short-term foster care;

• permanent foster care;

• kinship foster care;

• concurrent foster care;

• private foster care.

The first four categories are types of fostering which apply to children in the looked after system and will be discussed further below. Private fostering is an arrangement between the families concerned and although covered by the Children Act 1989 under section 66 little was known about it, with limited research being carried out in this area (Wilson et al, 2004). Private fostering is an area though of considerable concern, particularly since the case of Victoria Climbié who was privately fostered. There have been changes post Climbié which seek to offer more protection to privately fostered children, section 44 of the Children Act 2004 introduced national minimum standards for private fostering arrangements. Placements are now subject to regulation through the Children (Private Arrangements for Fostering) Regulations 2005. Replacement practice guidance (also introduced in 2005) strengthens and enhances the previous Children Act 1989 guidance by seeking to focus the attention of local authorities on private fostering by requiring them to be more proactive. Many now have dedicated workers for private fostering however the scope of their role does seem to vary from authority to authority.

What provision for monitoring and supporting private fostering arrangements are there in your local area? Do these arrangements comply with the practice guidance?

Short-term foster care

This provides a service for the many children who enter the looked after system for a short time. There were around 32,000 short-term fostered children in 2000/1 at any one time, with a similar number leaving the system (Department of Health, 2001). More recent statistics (Department for Education and Skills 2006) no longer provide this total so comparisons are difficult however as there is little difference in other categories similarities may well remain. Among the children who left the looked after system just under a third spent less than eight weeks in the system, 43 per cent less than six months. Of the children who remain in the LAC system 65 per cent who have been looked after for more than six months are likely to stay in the system for more than four years (Department of Health, 1999). Short-term fostering is used for a variety of purposes, for example:

- in an emergency to safeguard a young child of three months who has fractures where there are no apparent medical reasons or satisfactory explanations;

- where a parent has been admitted to hospital in an emergency and there is no one to care for the child;

- when a parent and baby are being assessed to see if their parenting is of a safe standard;

- where a young person has been remanded to the care of the local authority pending trial for offences.

Permanent foster care

Provides children who, for whatever reason, cannot either live with their parents or be placed for adoption with continuity of care throughout their remaining childhood. Adoption is not appropriate for all children and young people: they may have significant relationships within their birth families, they may wish for permanence but without severing legal relationships. Special Guardianship Orders (which gives Special Guardians parental responsibility and the ability to make decisions about children in most areas of their lives, whether their parents agree or not) are an option available to long term foster carers. These orders remove children from the Looked After system but do not sever their legal relationship with their birth family. They do give them security, and their carers parental responsibility, in their placement.

Kinship foster care

This is provided for looked after children by relatives and friends, however without having parental responsibility for the child. Children who are subject to care orders can be placed with relatives or friends after an appropriate assessment. Allowances are usually paid for this type of fostering but at a lesser rate than non-relative foster carers. Support for kinship carers varies, research (Hunt, Waterhouse and Lutman, 2007) reaffirms the need for careful assessment and adequate support if such placements are to realise their potential for children. Special Guardianship is also an option for kinship carers where it is felt by the courts to be appropriate.

Concurrent foster care

These placements are a comparatively recent development within the UK. In these placements a child is placed with foster carers who are both approved foster carers and approved adopters. The child is usually the subject of court proceedings where there are ongoing assessments and efforts to try to return the child to their parents. However, if these are not successful then the foster carers, as approved adopters, can apply to adopt the child. There are high expectations of foster carers in these situations. They must have a positive approach to the assessment processes, which are likely to involve frequent contact, whilst maintaining a commitment to the child as a potentially permanent family member. Such situations require a high level of support for the carers if they are to fulfil these roles which are potentially in conflict.

Regulations

Fostering placements for looked after children are provided by local authorities, independent fostering organisations and voluntary organisations under section 59 of the Children Act 1989. Fostering provision is made subject to the Fostering Service Regulations 2002 and the National Minimum Fostering Standards 2002 (in addition to those for private fostering mentioned above). The regulations cover all aspects of fostering including the conduct of agencies as well as the assessment, approval and support of foster carers. The minimum standards are qualitative, but intended to be measurable and are grouped in eight areas as follows:

- statement of purpose;
- fitness to carry on or manage a fostering service;
- management of a fostering service;
- securing and promoting welfare;
- recruiting, checking, managing, supporting and training staff and foster carers;
- records;
- fitness of premises;
- financial requirements.

The legal basis for fostering is found in the Children Act 1989, but this has been further developed by subsequent policy and further legislation. The Quality Protects 1998 and Choice Protects, 2003, initiatives, the *National Standards for Foster Care 2002*, the *Children (Leaving Care) Act 2000* and the *DfEE / DoH Guidance on the Education of Children and Young People in Public Care* have the underlying purpose of promoting and safeguarding the welfare of children and young people as well as an emphasis on their involvement in decisions which affect them.

The process of fostering

Fostering begins with the initial contact with prospective carers and involves assessment, approval, referral, matching, support and review processes. See Figure 6.1 for an illustration of these processes.

The assessment and approval of foster carers

All foster carers, apart from those who are fostering privately, go through a process which both assesses and prepares them to foster. Some agencies use the Fostering Network's assessment package, others might use the British Association of Adoption and Fostering's Form F, others devise their own, however all cover the same essential areas. The majority of agencies employ specialist, experienced workers to undertake these tasks.

Both fostering and adoption assessments consider whether applicants have the 'competence' to meet the needs of children through processes which although not identical are similar. See Figures 6.1 and 6.3. 'Competence' is assessed in the following areas:

- *Caring for children* This would include providing a good standard of physical and emotional care to children who will have experienced loss and who are likely to have been harmed as well as ensuring they receive appropriate education and health care.

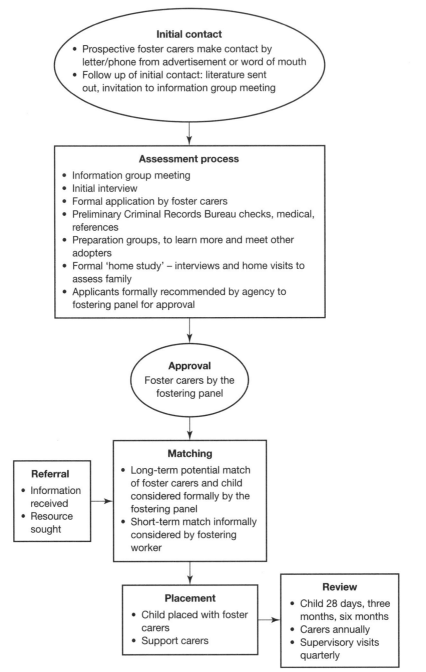

Figure 6.1 *The fostering process*

- *Providing a safe and caring environment* This would include providing a safe physical environment and keeping children safe from harm outside the home.

- *Working as part of a team* This would include the ability to keep information confidential, to work with other professional people and the child's family whether directly or indirectly through contact.

- *Carers' own past history and development* This would include looking at past experiences and how they impact on carers now, what have they learnt from these experiences and how they might impact on their ability to care for a child.

In addition to the competence assessment fostering and adoption assessments undertake statutory checks with a number of agencies including the police, the health authority and social services as well as a full medical examination. For further information see www.baaf.org.uk and www.fostering.net.

All the information about prospective foster carers is presented to a fostering panel, (see Figure 6.2, which has to make a recommendation to the agency as to whether or not the applicant(s) should be *approved* as a carer(s). As with adoption panels all recommendations are considered by a decision-maker (a senior manager) within the agency for final approval. Agency decision-makers normally agree with the panel's decision although this is not always the case. Further information about panel functions is contained within the Fostering Service Regulations, 2002.

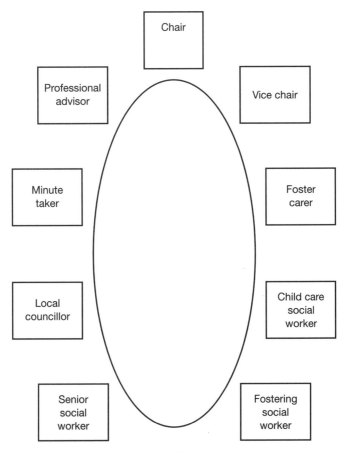

Figure 6.2 *An example of the composition of a Fostering Panel*

The following case study, which has already been introduced to you in previous chapters, will now be used to highlight the various processes you may be involved in as a social worker in a fostering team.

CASE STUDY

A referral has been made for foster care for three children, Kylie Cole aged 12 who is African-Caribbean/White and has learning disabilities, Tariq Khan aged 3, African-Caribbean/Asian and Nadia Khan aged 1, African-Caribbean/Asian. Donna Green aged 26 is living with her partner Ahmed Khan, the father of the two youngest children Tariq and Nadia. The eldest child, Kylie, has contact with her father Alan Cole aged 28. The reason for the referral is neglect of Kylie, subsequently there are allegations of sexual abuse. Both younger children are found to be neglected with later injuries found on Nadia (fractures). This case study will enable you to consider the processes of fostering by working through the activities below.

The referral process

This can be thought of as the collation of key information in order to obtain a service or resource, which in this instance is a foster home. Activity 6.3 will help you to understand the referral process.

ACTIVITY 6.3

What information do you think is needed when a referral is received for foster care? Is there a minimum amount of information that you would need to help you to place the children with suitable foster carers?

Comment

This should include the full names of the children, ages and dates of birth, current address; ethnic, racial and religious background; details of any school or nurseries attending; general practitioner (GP); details of parents and other carer or person with whom the children have contact.

What about diet, any allergies, medication needed? Would this subsequent information be easy to obtain and from whom would you obtain the information? How would you obtain this information, who do you think would best provide this sort of detail about a child's life? Ideally you would obtain information from parents, relatives, friends, or carers, however other professionals such as health visitors, GPs and teachers may also be useful sources.

ACTIVITY 6.4

Look back at the case study and consider:

Do you think Kylie has been neglected? If she has how might this affect the kind of foster placement that will best meet her needs and indeed the needs of the other children? Can all of the three children's needs be met in one foster placement? Do you think that there are sufficient resources available to enable you to place all three children together?

Comment

These are complex issues, which may require further assessment and consultation with other professionals. Iwaniec (1995) provides a good introduction to the identification, assessment and the intervention and treatment of the emotionally abused and neglected child. Iwaniec defines neglect as:

> the passive ignoring of a child's emotional needs, a lack of attention and stimulation, parental unavailability to care, supervise, guide, teach and protect .

She gives a helpful account of how to identify emotional abuse and neglect including such issues as non-organic failure to thrive, the failure to grow and develop healthily. It refers to children whose weight, height and general development are significantly below the expected norms (see Chapter 4 for further discussion).

The matching process

This can be thought of as assembling or linking two sets of information with each other in order to make a placement decision, which is beneficial to both the children and carers. The information about the children which is contained on the referral is matched or linked with the information about the foster carers.

ACTIVITY **6.5**

What information might you need to know about the foster family before you place all of these children within them?

Comment

The information that you might need to know would include the following:

- Which foster carers have vacancies?

- How many children are they approved for and what is the age range of the child or children that they are approved for?

- What experience do the carers have of caring for children?

- Can the children share a bedroom or is there a need for separate bedroom accommodation?

- Do the foster carers share the children's ethnic, racial and religious background?

- Some estimate of the length of time the foster placement is needed would also be helpful.

- Is the foster placement in a geographical area that is easily accessible for family, friends and relatives and school or nursery?

- How will the placements of the children affect the foster carer's own children and their position within the foster family?

- Finally, would the order of this list be different if the foster placement was being requested on a Monday as opposed to a Friday afternoon?

Each fostering agency would have a centrally held information resource, which you would need to access. This could be through a duty social worker but practice will vary from agency to agency. Subject to there being appropriate carers available you would then contact the fostering social worker or the carers directly to obtain the information needed and then decide whether to place the children. The realities of practice mean that there may be little choice or that children may be placed, in emergency, with carers who do not match their needs. Systems which operate out of office hours will again vary from agency to agency, for example some are covered by emergency duty teams who cover all provisions whereas others have on-call social workers and/or 'buddy' foster carers.

The support process

As the fostering social worker your task is to support the foster carers. This involves sharing the burden by giving additional assistance in the form of physical, financial and psychological support. The support starts by sharing the initial information from the referral. Support for the carers continues with a discussion with the foster carers of the children's needs and the provision of any financial or physical support that the foster carer may need. Providing psychological support involves thinking about the needs of others, including their feelings and emotions and offering appropriate assistance.

ACTIVITY **6.6**

How important is this support to the foster carer? What impact would having three extra people staying with you have on your family? Think about what the foster carers might need immediately in order to care for a 1, 3 and 12-year-old?

Comment

The first considerations may well be around practicalities, for example who would provide the money to buy nappies, clothes, appropriate food, some toys, appropriate bedding, buggies, cot etc? Who would you expect to obtain these items? If the carer, would the carer's transport be adequate? Will the carers have the time? How would the eldest child get to school? How would the carer manage to take their own children to school as well as the foster children? If the children are separated and placed in different foster homes are the carers given each other's contact numbers? How much ongoing support will be required to ensure that the children's basic needs continue to be met? As well as dealing with the day-to-day care of the children the foster carers also need to be encouraged to keep a record of any changes in the children's behaviour. If you are supporting them well you will need to ensure that they have the means to record this information. Finally, how much support should foster carers be given? Is 9 a.m. to 5 p.m. adequate or should they receive 24-hour support and, if this is the case, should that support be shared between their fostering agency and a network of other carers? In any case should foster carers be paid properly for the work they do or should they continue to receive an allowance?

Being able to offer appropriate support involves having the knowledge to know when to intervene, the skill to know how to intervene and the reason why you are intervening.

The review process

This involves examining the previous process and the care that the children are currently receiving. The views of the children and others should be sought and recorded as part of the review process. Decisions are made regarding whether the foster placement should continue or alternative care provision should be sought. The safety and well-being of the children is paramount and the review should address whether the behaviour of the child gives any cause for concern such as sexualised or aggressive behaviour towards self or others. The review should be chaired by an Independent Reviewing Officer as outlined in the Review of Children's Cases (Amendment) (England) Regulations 2004 and also take into account the statutory guidance which was also issued in 2004. The legislation relating to Independent Reviewing Officers was introduced by section 118 of Adoption and Children Act 2002 . The review will also consider if there has there been any improvement or deterioration in the children's behaviour or conduct? When has this occurred?

We hope that by working through some of the questions you have been able to imagine that you are the fostering social worker and indeed the foster carer. We also hope that you have managed to analyse the processes involved and think about how much time, energy and effort might be devoted to the different parts of the process. Finally, and most importantly, that the next activity will help you to think about how you might feel as one of the children in the process.

ACTIVITY **6.7**

How would you feel if you were suddenly transported to live with people you did not know, in a place that was unfamiliar, where none of the certainties you knew existed anymore? How would you be?

Comment

The healing process begins with the recognition of pain and hurt and the re-establishment of routines that give meaning, purpose and pleasure to life, and the long-term provision of care, patience, stability, understanding and love, as the potential stability of fostering and the permanence of adoption can provide.

RESEARCH SUMMARY

Innovative, Tried and Tested: A Review of Good Practice in Fostering (Sellick and Howell, 2003) provides a helpful summary of key areas which children, carers, social workers and agencies identify as important for key messages for good practice.

Key messages

- Many fostering agencies are using research evidence to make recruitment effective: local recruitment schemes, for example word of mouth and brief articles in the local press, achieve success.

- There is innovative training practice, consistent with research evidence, about what carers say that they want: managing contacts dealing with children's behaviour, and supporting children's education.

- Information and Communication Technology (ICT) is playing an increasingly important role in key areas: training, information and user evaluation.

- Agencies are developing a wide range of retention schemes, for example loyalty payments, 'buddying' arrangements, stress management and services for carers' own children.

- Some agencies are providing carers with career choices within or connected to fostering. The benefits include retaining carers, using their skills flexibly and increasing their job satisfaction.

- Partnership working and commissioning enables many agencies to improve the availability of both general and specialised placements.

- There is evidence of the growing development of specialist placements for children with complex and special needs, some of which have been researched and evaluated.

- Many agencies now offer additional services to help the children placed; foster carers themselves are satisfied when children and young people they care for receive them.

- Fostered children and young people are consulted quite often; however, their opinions are rarely communicated to senior managers or elected members to inform policy.

- Foster carers participate in the evaluation of many aspects of fostering services.

- Parents and other relatives of fostered children are given few opportunities to participate in shaping fostering services.

(Sellick and Howell, 2003)

Adoption

Adoption as an informal arrangement has existed for many years, but its history in law is much shorter. Prior to the first adoption act, the Adoption of Children Act 1926, birth parents could legally demand the return of their children even though they had been cared for in another family for many years. This Act was the first which allowed for the transfer of the rights and obligations in respect of a child from birth parents to adopters, and also gave courts the power to dispense with the agreement of birth parents in some circumstances. Subsequent legislation followed which built on this Act until the current legislation was introduced in 1976.

Adoption is the legal transfer of parental responsibility from birth parent(s) to adoptive parent(s). This is the only process which permanently removes parental responsibility from the birth parent(s) and gives it to another parent(s). Adoption also has the effect of removing parental responsibility from local authorities. Adoption can be through agreement, for example for a baby whose parent is unable to care for them or through compulsion against the wishes of the birth parent, usually where a child has been made the subject of a care order. Adoption procedures take place under the Adoption and

Children Act 2002 (ACA 2002) which was fully implemented in December 2005 (some parts of the act had already been implemented piecemeal over the preceeding years). The ACA 2002 was drafted following the *Quality Protects* initiative (DoH 1998), and the *Performance and Innovation Unit of the Cabinet Report* in 2000. Both of these publications considered reforms to adoption, although there had already been a previous adoption bill published in 1993. The previous law was felt to be out of step with the Children Act 1989, there were concerns that there were children waiting for adoption and that too many applicants were unsuccessful.

ACA 2002 has changed the process of adoption by introducing placement orders which are required before a child can be placed for adoption without parental consent, it has also made adoption accessible to couples who are not married and those who have civil partnerships, adoption continues to be available to single people and to step parents.

Table 6.3 *Looked after children adopted during the years ending 31 March by gender, age at adoption, ethnic origin, category of need, final legal status, duration of final period of care and age on starting final period of care, 2003–2007*[1,2]

England   numbers and percentages

	numbers					percentages				
	2003	2004	2005	2006	2007	2003	2004	2005	2006	2007
All looked after children[1]	61,200	61,200	61,000	60,300	60,000					
All Children looked after adopted[1]	3,500	3,800	3,800	3,700	3,300	100	100	100	100	100
Gender	3,500	3,800	3,800	3,700	3,300	100	100	100	100	100
Male	1,900	1,900	1,900	1,900	1,700	53	51	51	51	50
Female	1,700	1,900	1,800	1,800	1,600	47	49	49	49	50
Age at adoption (years)	3,500	3,800	3,800	3,700	3,300	100	100	100	100	100
Under 1	220	220	210	200	150	6	6	6	5	5
1 to 4	2,200	2,200	2,300	2,400	2,100	62	58	62	64	64
5 to 9	960	1,100	1,100	950	880	27	30	28	26	27
10 to 15	180	210	160	180	160	5	6	4	5	5
16 and over	10	20	20	20	10	0	0	0	0	0
Average age (yrs: months)	4:4	4:5	4:2	4:1	4:2					
Ethnic origin	3,500	3,800	3,800	3,700	3,300	100	100	100	100	100
White	3,100	3,200	3,200	3,200	2,800	87	86	86	85	85
Mixed	290	330	350	380	340	8	9	9	10	10
Asian or Asian British	40	50	50	50	60	1	1	1	1	2
Black or Black British	90	100	80	90	90	2	3	2	2	3
Other ethnic groups	40	50	40	30	30	1	1	1	1	1
Category of need[3]	3,500	3,800	3,800	3,700	3,300	100	100	100	100	100
Abuse or neglect	2,600	2,800	2,800	2,700	2,400	75	74	74	74	74
Child's disability	30	30	30	20	20	1	1	1	1	1
Parents illness or disability	200	160	190	180	160	6	4	5	5	5
Family in acute distress	170	230	220	230	160	5	6	6	6	5
Family dysfunction	290	290	340	310	310	8	8	9	8	9
Socially unacceptable behaviour	10	–	–	10	–	0	–	–	0	–
Low income	0	–	–	10	–	0	–	–	0	–
Absent parenting	210	260	200	190	190	6	7	5	5	6

Table 6.3 *(continued)*

England   **numbers and percentages**

	numbers					percentages				
	2003	2004	2005	2006	2007	2003	2004	2005	2006	2007
Final legal status	**3,500**	**3,800**	**3,800**	**3,700**	**3,300**	**100**	**100**	**100**	**100**	**100**
Freed for adoption[4]	1,500	1,700	1,900	1,900	1,200	42	44	49	51	38
Placement Order[5]	x	x	x	20	630	x	x	x	0	19
Care order	1,700	1,700	1,600	1,500	1,200	48	46	42	41	36
Voluntary agreement (S20)	350	370	340	280	230	10	10	9	8	7
Duration of final period of care[6]	**3,500**	**3,800**	**3,800**	**3,700**	**3,300**	**100**	**100**	**100**	**100**	**100**
Under 1 year	250	260	260	240	170	7	7	7	6	5
1 year to under 2 years	1,200	1,300	1,400	1,400	1,200	35	33	36	38	36
2 years to under 3 years	960	1,100	1,100	1,100	980	27	28	30	30	30
3 years and over	1,100	1,200	1,000	950	970	31	32	27	26	29
Average duration (yrs: mths)	2:9	2:8	2:7	2:7	2:8					
Age on starting final period of care (years)[6]	**3,500**	**3,800**	**3,800**	**3,700**	**3,300**	**100**	**100**	**100**	**100**	**100**
Under 1	2,000	2,000	2,100	2,100	1,900	56	53	56	57	58
1	440	470	470	470	370	13	12	13	13	11
2	380	400	400	340	360	11	11	11	9	11
3	280	310	300	270	250	8	8	8	7	8
4 and over	450	580	500	510	420	13	15	13	14	13
Average age (yrs: mths)	1:7	1:8	1:7	1:7	1:6					

1. Source: SSDA903 return on children looked after.
2. Historical data may differ from older publications. This is mainly due to the implementation of amendments and corrections sent by some local authorities after the publication date of previous materials.
3. The most applicable category of the eight "Need Codes" (i.e. the reason why the child is receiving social services) at the time the child was taken into care rather than necessarily the reason they are looked after.
4. No new applications for freeing orders may be made on or after 30 December 2005.
5. Placement orders came into force on 30 December 2005.
6. "Period of care" refers to a continuous period of being looked after, which may include more than one placement or legal status.

Inspite of the introduction of ACA 2002 there has been a decrease in the numbers of children looked after who have been adopted in 2006 and 2007 (see Table 6.3). Some of the decrease may have been caused by the use of Special Guardianship orders but further research is needed before this change can be fully evaluated. The majority of children adopted remain in the 1 to 9 age group which contrasts with the figures in Table 6.1 for children and young people generally in the looked after system.

The process of adoption

Adoption, like fostering, begins with the initial contact with prospective carers and involves assessment, approval, referral, matching, support and review processes. (See Figure 6.3 for an illustration of these processes.)

Adoption also involves the permanent transfer of parental responsibility to an adoptive parent or parents. As you will have seen in Chapter 4 Kylie, Tariq and Nadia came into the looked after system following allegations of abuse. They have now been made the subject of care orders and have been placed in foster care. The task for the social worker is to meet the needs of each individual child. Adoption can be thought of as permanent substitute care and is a way of achieving a more stable, secure life for a child. It is a way of severing the birth parental responsibilities and creating a new legal adoptive parental responsibility. Adoption involves making difficult decisions. In this instance the decision is made to separate Kylie from her younger siblings.

Vera Fahlberg provides an excellent guide to the child's experience in care and the management of their journey in *A Child's Journey through Placement* (2004).

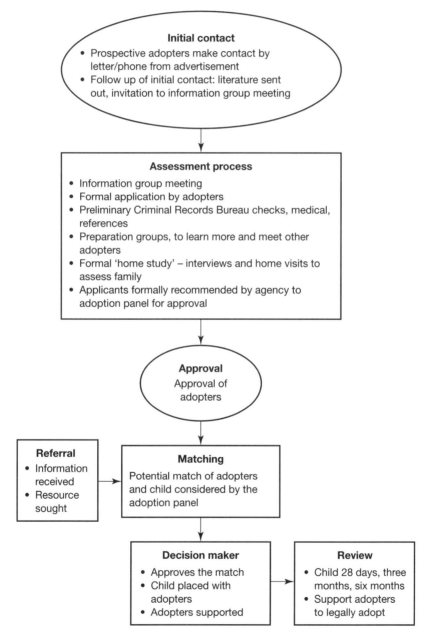

Figure 6.3 The adoption process

The referral process

This begins with a decision that Tariq's and Nadia's needs would be best met by being placed for adoption together, following the s47 investigation and court proceedings discussed in Chapter 4. Tariq and Nadia are then referred to the adoption agencies as children who need adoptive parents. Information about each child is assembled using the Child's Permanence Report (CPR) This is a method of collating extensive information about the child and their family including development, life history, medical, education, family details, any harm experienced and special needs. Following the implementation of ACA 2002 there is some variation in format but the information should be the same. A similar process is undertaken for adoptive parents, the information is prepared using the British Association of Adoption and Fostering's Form F. The children's social worker would prepare the documentation for Tariq and Nadia, the adoption worker for the adoptive parent(s).

Consider the following:

- What issues might the children's social worker face when collecting information about the children if the parents are not in agreement with the plan for adoption?

- If the parents are co-operating with the plan, how reliable is the information which they are giving you?

- Is there any influential involvement from relatives that might assist the information gathering process or slow it down?

- Are there any legal considerations that need to be taken into account?

- How would things be different if consent to the adoption was agreed?

- How would things be different if consent was withheld?

- How would you check the accuracy of the information?

The matching process

For adoption this can be thought of as assembling or linking two sets of information with each other in order to make a placement decision, which is beneficial to both the children and adopters. Before this linking can occur the children, Tariq and Nadia, have to be recommended as suitable for adoption by an adoption panel. The panel must consist of at least five members and no more than ten members. They include at least:

- one man and one woman;

- an independent chair person;

- a vice chair person (one of the panel members);

- two social workers in the employment of the adoption agency;

- a member of the local authority's social services committee/executive/overview and scrutiny committee covering social services functions or a voluntary adoption agency management representative;

- the agency medical adviser;

- at least three members who are independent of the agency; this should include where practical an adoptive parent and an adopted person aged over 18;
- other members could include a representative of a Black or minority ethnic group;
- a disabled person;
- a parent;
- a doctor with special interest in child health;
- a health visitor;
- a teacher or educational psychologist;
- a probation officer;
- a social worker from another adoption agency (DoH, 2002).

A typical example of an adoption panel is represented in Figure 6.4

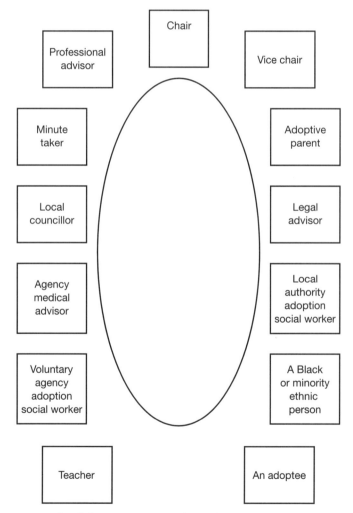

Figure 6.4 *An example of the composition of an adoption panel*

The adoption panel will also have a legal advisor who provides advice on all the legal aspects of applications from prospective adopters, children recommended for placement for adoption and the matching process. There will also be a professional advisor from the agency to provide advice and practice procedure. Adoption panels, as with fostering panels, make recommendations, which also have to be confirmed by the agency decision-maker.

ACTIVITY **6.8**

Can adopters attend the panels in the agencies? What factors do you think may prevent adopters from attendance at the panel?

Comment

All agencies should facilitate prospective adopters attending panels, many provide information about the process and membership to help prepare people for the experience though it can still be a stressful experience for them.

Think about what 'criteria of suitability' the adoption panel might use when recommending that Tariq and Nadia should be placed for adoption. The panel will offer advice to the child's social worker about applying for a placement order (to enable the child to be placed with prospective adopters), contact arrangements with birth families and any matching criteria which might be relevant. The adoptive parents also have to be approved as suitable adopters The panel consider age, health, parenting capacity/potential, ethnic/racial/cultural background, religion and motivation. What else do you think might be included?

Do you think space, time, energy and commitment from the adopters are just as important?

As well as recommending that children should be placed for adoption and adopters as suitable adoptive parents, adoption panels also recommend approval of the match between the approved adoptive parents and children who should be placed for adoption. The process of matching is much more rigorous and complex, as you would expect when attempting to ensure that the adopters will be able to meet the needs of the child for life. Panels have to consider some complex and controversial issues. These may be grouped as follows:

- Issues about the child's birth family such as mental illness, which the adopters may well have some difficulty accepting.

- The wishes and feelings of the birth family about the type of adoptive family the child should be placed with might be unrealistic.

- The child's current understanding of, and feelings about, the past and about what is planned might not have been known fully due to the child's age and level of understanding.

- Identity issues are sometimes in conflict with attachment issues.

- Is a same race placement more important than being able to make an attachment to a carer?

- How accepting or otherwise are the adopters of:
  - abuse and neglect issues, behavioural issues
  - health and disability issues
  - education issues
  - contact issues
  - the needs of siblings
  - other children in the new family
  - any financial issues and their own feelings and expectations.

Many of these issues should have already been explored in general with the prospective adopters during the assessment. The social workers for the child and the adopters (usually two different people, possibly from different agencies) will explore how the children's needs can be met, focusing on the issues which are relevant in more depth prior to the match going to the adoption panel. The panel will consider all the information about the child and the prospective adoptive family as well as a report detailing why this is felt to be an appropriate match and what support will be offered following placement. A fuller account is given of these issues in Lord and Cullen (2006); Byrne (2000) also offers helpful advice on linking children with new families prior to placement. The panel considers the support plan and can offer advice about any aspect of this including contact, financial support, therapeutic input and the delegation of parental responsibility which occurs in restricted form when the child is placed with the prospective adopters.

The support process

Generally, three periods of support can be identified within the process: pre-approval, pre-adoption and post-adoption. The pre-approval phase includes the period of initial assessment of suitability. The pre-adoption stage includes the period from approval by the adoption panel to the granting of an adoption order and the post-adoption period includes the period after an adoption order has been granted. Adopters should receive support during the assessment process or pre-approval phase. What form do you think this support might take? Usually adopters are either encouraged to continue with the process or they are discouraged from continuing. The pre-adoption phase is usually characterised by intensive activity. The adopters have been approved, they have also been matched to a child by the adoption panel and the child has usually been placed. Adopters at this stage are surrounded by people, the adoption worker, the child's social worker, health visitors, all of whom are generally wanting to be helpful. What core skills, knowledge and values would you have used up to this point?

Comment

You will have used your preparatory skills to communicate verbally and in writing with many of the above people. You will have used your relationship building skills to form an open, honest and trusting relationship with the prospective adopters. You will have used your assessment skills to determine the suitability of the prospective adopters and explored the risks and benefits of the match. You will have used your knowledge of safeguarding children to inform, assess and clarify the prospective adopters' expectations of an adopted child. You will have valued the contributions of the prospective adopters and helped them to understand the value and usefulness of their positive and negative life experiences.

Other types of support have been offered to adopters, including contact with birth families as well as supporting adopted children to enable them to obtain access to their birth records.

The Adoption and Children Act 2002 has addressed some of the issues around the variable provision of support services by requiring an adoption support plan for all placements, this should mean some improvement in the services provided for adoptive families . There does however remain a central problem because although all adopters are entitled to an assessment of need for their children (a duty under the Act) there is only a power to provide services, leaving this at the discretion of the local authority.

The review process

During this process you might want to consider how Tariq and Nadia have settled since being placed with their adoptive parents. What specific factors would you want to examine? Have the children established a routine? Have they begun to make an attachment to their new carers and have they begun to detach themselves from their previous carers? Do they sleep well or are they awake during the night? Are they eating well? How are Tariq and Nadia getting on together? Do you as the adoption worker share the social worker's assessment? Is there any contact with any siblings? A decision was made to separate Kylie from her siblings, Tariq and Nadia. Kylie has been placed in residential care. A brief discussion of this form of substitute care will be outlined.

Residential care

The majority of children in the LAC system are placed in foster care or for adoption, however, around 11 per cent of children are cared for in residential settings. Residential care is provided by local authorities, voluntary and independent agencies. All residential homes for children must be registered and inspected by OFSTED through its review processes. This percentage has remained static for the last four years (see Table 6.2). Statistics from the Department of Health published in 2007 indicated that these figures had fallen since 2003 and that there had also been a fall in local authority maintained homes. There had, however, been an increase in the number of privately registered homes.

Over the course of many years there have been concerns about the abuse of power in residential children's homes (Levy and Kahan, 1991; the Warner report, 1992). Further and more recent concerns have led to a number of inquiries, including that of Utting, 1991 and Waterhouse, 1997 which considered the safeguarding of children living away from home and the scandal of abuse in children's homes in Wales respectively. These inquiries identified the need to ensure that children could be safely cared for in residential care by promoting minimum standards and ensuring appropriate staffing. Additional national occupational standards were introduced for managers in residential childcare, ToPSS,

2003, to try to ensure all children's homes meet the requirements of the National Minimum Care Standards for Children's Homes, 2001 and the Children's Homes Regulations, 2001.

All these seek to ensure that children and young people receive appropriate and safe care by addressing a wide range of issues. These range from requiring each home to have a statement of purpose, placement plans for children and regular reviews on privacy, personal appearance, and the provision and preparation of meals. All areas of a child's life have a minimum standard which homes are assessed against. In theory this should mean that a child or young person should have their needs met in a similar way wherever they are in England.

RESEARCH SUMMARY

Unsworth (2004) found, in her review of how care services provide information in relation to National Minimum Standards of care homes in England, that there were still disparities between homes. Nineteen % (representing about 280 homes) did not meet the standard required to provide information, the majority (59%) almost met it, 21% did meet it and 2% exceeded it. She also found that where there was good practice there was no significant difference by provider type and that only one region was significantly worse than the rest. Good practice in children's homes is shown through service user guides, in easy to understand and appropriate language, which are actually used. It is further indicated by service user involvement in creating statements of purpose and guides and the use of appropriate formats. (Unsworth, 2004). Choice, Power and Performance: The need for information on care services in England. The Stationery Office.

Some of the concerns which have arisen about residential care and indeed children in the looked after system generally have been the inability of children and young people to be listened to and heard. Efforts are being made to address this in different ways and to build upon the Children Act 1989 which has clear statements on ascertaining the child's wishes and feelings.

Complaints procedures for children and young people were introduced by the Act to provide a formal process for services users to either complain or express their views. These have been updated by the Advocacy Services and Representations Procedure (Children) (Amendment) Regulations 2004 to try to ensure that children and young people are listened to when they wish to formally express a view or make a complaint and that they have access to an independent advocate to support them if they wish.

Residential care can be used for a number of purposes including short-term care for children with disabilities. The majority of residential provision is for young people with challenging behaviour for whom foster care is either not appropriate or has not been successful (Colton, Sanders and Williams, 2001).

Homes are staffed by teams of people who provide care for the children and young people. The majority of homes have rotas with staff working shifts, information being shared through change over meetings or by daily logs of events. Issues can arise if teams do not take the same approach with service users, which can result in inconsistent care. Young people can also find it difficult to relate to teams and struggle if their key worker is not available when they need them. Conversely others prefer this setting because it is less like family life, as for example in a foster home. In addition to the average sized eight bedded home larger units do exist. Some provide secure accommodation for young people who are considered to be putting themselves at risk and have been placed there by court order. These units also accommodate young people who are either on remand for, or have been convicted of, serious criminal offences. For further discussion see Johns, 2007 Chapter 6.

CASE STUDY

Kylie is unable to remain in her foster home. Her behaviour has become very challenging, she has started to steal money from the foster carers and has assaulted their 12 year-old son. She has also begun to stay out at night and has been seen with a man who is thought to deal in drugs and act as a pimp for young girls. You need to find Kylie an alternative placement, how will you go about this and what will influence you?

Summary

All children's homes should have a statement of purpose, which may be a good starting point in your discussions with Kylie. The minimum standards may also be useful as would any inspection reports about the home. You will need to find out Kylie's views, taking them into account whilst balancing them with her welfare and best interests.

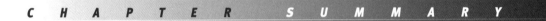

C   H   A   P   T   E   R   S   U   M   M   A   R   Y

This chapter will help you to meet the subject benchmark 3.2.2, which requires you to develop problem-solving skills. You have been introduced to the concept of substitute care for children and young people. The chapter has outlined the structure which underlies the provision of services and has considered the processes involved in them. The chapter has also given you the opportunity of beginning to work through and reflect upon the complexities and dilemmas that arise in successful substitute care for children.

FURTHER
READING

Cockburn, V (ed.) (2000) *It's mad that's all: A collection of poems about being looked after*. London: Foster Carers Association.
Poems from young people in the looked after system in which young people express their feelings about all aspects of life.

Fahlberg, V (2004) *A child's journey through placement*. London: British Association for Adoption and Fostering.
A classic text on the experience of children in the looked after system which includes child development, separation and loss, attachment and direct work with children.

Salter, A N (2004) *The adopters' handbook: Information, resources and services for adoptive parents.* London: British Association for Adoption and Fostering.

Sellick, C and Howell, D (2003) *Innovative, tried and tested: A review of good practice in fostering.* London: Social Care Institute for Excellence.
This text describes good innovative practice in fostering in the context of findings from research.

Conclusion

This book has sought to introduce you to social work practice with children and families through discussion of the context of the work and how that work can be carried out. We have done this by focussing on differing aspects of practice and by introducing a case study to highlight social workers involvement with children and families as a basis for further exploration.

Chapter one introduced you to some of the issues and dilemmas which you will face when working with children and families. This chapter will assist your understanding and appreciation of how values and ethics influence social work practice with children and families. This is a complex area of work which requires much personal self-evaluation and reflection; this chapter will have helped you to begin that process. The activities in the chapter have been designed to encourage you to think about how personal, professional, agency and societal values can influence social work practice with children and families. As you have worked through the activities we also hope that you will be able to make the links between the national occupational standards that social workers need to meet, particularly Key Role 6, and to demonstrate professional competence. In addition, we also hope that you have been able to identify the social processes that can lead to marginalisation, isolation and exclusion which in turn lead to families needing support. This chapter also sought to start you thinking about developing your problem-solving skills by taking account of the impact of discrimination: personal, professional, agency and societal. Thinking about how values and ethics impact on your practice will also help you to develop a solid value base which will, we hope, help you to become a reflective, anti-oppressive and empowering practitioner.

Chapter two, in considering the historical and policy context as a starting point for practice with children and families, gives context to the work, giving you a sense of how working with children and families has changed over time. This chapter provides a foundation for working within Key Roles 2, 3 and 6 as well as an introduction to some of the issues which have arisen, for example, within child death inquiries and the treatment of children in the Looked After system. Finally the chapter has tried to help you consider the forthcoming changes in social work with children and families which have resulted primarily from the Climbié and other recent inquiries.

Chapter three further develops your foundation for working within Key Roles 1, 2, 3 and 4 by introducing you to ideas around supportive and preventative social work. These ideas have become embodied in government policies such as Home and Sure Start, the promotion of Family Centres and the more recent developments encompassed in *Every Child Matters*. Definitions of family support were discussed to help gain an understanding of how the concept has developed over time. The chapter also considered the characteristics of family support and related areas of social work practice together with how needs are defined and the importance of the assessment process. The chapter then raised your awareness of the need for the planning and reviewing of any intervention in ways which are sensitive to the individual circumstances of children and their families. Additionally, the chapter provided you with case examples of family support interventions for different problems and outcomes to enable you to relate the theory to practice examples. These discussions will provide you with a sound basis to develop your social work practice and meet the relevant quality assurance benchmarks.

Finally this chapter highlights the importance of this work and acknowledges how early intervention can prevent situations deteriorating to the point when there is little option but to take a much more interventionist approach.

Chapter four will provide a foundation for meeting all the Key Roles by focussing on the skills and knowledge needed by social workers to work effectively with children and families within the safeguarding children arena. It outlined the categories and definitions of child abuse before introducing you to the issues being addressed by safeguarding children practitioners throughout the country, particularly the impact of domestic violence, drug and alcohol problems and mental illness/distress on children.

The chapter then highlighted current legislation, policies, guidance, methods of intervention and the framework for assessing children and families using examples from practice in relation to the Cole/Green family to enhance your understanding. You were then introduced to the developments and changes in legislation, guidance and the assessment framework following the implementation of the Children Act 2004 and *Every Child Matters* (2003).

Finally the chapter helped you to consider safeguarding children as a high profile area of social work practice and what causes concerns about children's welfare. The chapter also highlighted the dilemmas of safeguarding children from harm, for example by their parent/s and protecting the privacy and respect for family life from over zealous state intervention, whilst you as a social worker consistently put the interests of the child first.

Chapter five led you into a discussion of a particular area of practice and reinforced the idea that as social workers you need to focus on seeing and working with the child rather than the disability. This chapter will have provided you with a basis for meeting Key Roles 1, 2, 5 and 6 by helping you consider some of the issues facing children with disabilities and their families. It will have also helped you to develop your understanding, knowledge and skills to enable you to work effectively to support children with disabilities within their communities.

Different models of disability were explored with emphasis on the social model to help you promote inclusive social work practice. The chapter also emphasised the centrality of the views of children with disabilities and their families, and disabled adults, to aid your understanding of some of the barriers to inclusion that disabled children face in their daily lives.

Finally the chapter considered the differing services offered to children with disabilities and their families including the important areas of education and transition.

The final chapter in the book considers the care of children who are living away from their birth families by discussing the Looked After Children system and by reviewing the three main areas of substitute care. This chapter again provides a foundation for meeting Key Roles 1, 5 and 6. You were introduced to the principles of adoption, fostering and residential care within the current legal and social policy context. The processes of adoption and fostering were outlined using case study material to highlight the skills you will need, especially in assessment. The chapter also discussed residential provision as the other area of substitute care, again using case material to highlight principles, procedures and processes. The chapter highlighted the importance of the review process for all children within the Looked After Children system by providing you with details and discussion as a basis for developing your practice.

Working with children and their families incorporates many aspects of social work practice, and this book focuses on four of these key areas. Through the use of case studies and other exercises you should have gained an understanding of family support, safeguarding children, working with children with disabilities and children in the Looked After system. The book has begun your introduction to the skills and knowledge you will need to develop in working with children and families, and it provides a foundation for you to build on in your future career.

Work with children and families is challenging but can be very rewarding, you will be practicing as a social worker at a time of change when there are exciting opportunities for significant improvements in the whole arena. We wish you well as you continue on your journey.

References

Adoption: The future (1993) Cm 2288 Nov 1993.

Adoption and Children Act (2002). London: The Stationery Office.

Aiming high for disabled children: Better support for families (2007) London: The Stationery Office

Aldgate, J and Tunstill, J (1995) *Making sense of section 17: Implementing services for children in need within the Children Act 1989.* London: HMSO.

Allen, N (2007) *Making sense of the new adoption law*. Lyme Regis: Russell House Publications.

Audit Commission (1994) *Seen but not heard: Co-ordinating community child health and social services for children in need*. London: HMSO.

Badinter, E (1981) *The myth of motherhood: An historical view of the maternal instinct*. New York: Macmillan.

Baker, A and Duncan, S (1985) Child sexual abuse: a study of prevalence in Great Britain. *Journal of Child Abuse and Neglect*, 9; pp457–67.

Baldwin, S (1985) *The costs of caring: Families with disabled children*. London: Routledge and Kegan Paul.

Barker, J & Hodes, D (2007) *The child in mind: A child protection handbook third edition*. Routledge

Barn, R (ed) (1993) *Working with Black children and adolescents in need*. London: British Association for Adoption and Fostering.

Barnes, C (1992) *Disabling imagery and the media*. Halifax: British Council of Disabled People/Ryburn Publishing.

Beckett, C and Maynard, A (2005) *Values and ethics in social work*. London: Sage.

Beckett, C (2007) *Child protection: An introduction*. Second Edition. Sage

Bell, M and Wilson, K (eds) (2003) *Practitioner's guide to working with families*. Hampshire: Palgrave Macmillan.

Beresford, B (1995) *Expert opinions: A survey of parents caring for a severely disabled child*. Bristol: The Policy Press.

Beresford, B (2006) *Housing and disabled children: A review of policy levers and opportunities*. York: Joseph Rowntree Foundation.

Beresford, B and Oldman, C. (2002) *Housing matters: National evidence relating to disabled children and their housing*. The Policy Press, Bristol.

Booth, C (1889) *The life and labour of the people of London*. London: Macmillan and Co.

Brammer, A (2006) *Social work law, second edition*. Pearson Longman.

British Association for Adoption and Fostering (1998) *Form F1.* London: British Association for Adoption and Fostering.

Butt, J (1998) 'Are we being served?' *Community Care*, 24–25.

Butt, J and Box, L (1998a) *Family centred: A study of the use of family centres by Asian families.* London: Race Equality Unit.

Butt, J and Box, L (1998b) Engage and provide. *Community Care*, 22–23.

Byrne, S (2000) *Linking and introductions: Helping children join adoptive families.* London: British Association for Adoption and Fostering.

Bywater, J and Jones, R (2000) *Sexuality and social work.* Exeter: Learning Matters.

Carers and Disabled Children Act (2004). London: The Stationery Office.

Carers (Equal Opportunities) Act (2004). London: The Stationery Office.

Chand, A (2000) Over-representation of Black children in the child protection system. *Journal of Child and Family Social Work*, Volume 5, pp67–77.

Children Act (1948) London: Her Majesty's Stationery Office.

Children Act (1989) London: Her Majesty's Stationery Office.

Children Act (2004) London: The Stationery Office.

Children (Leaving Care) Act (2000) London: The Stationery Office.

Clark, CL (2000) *Social work ethics: Politics, principles and practice.* Basingstoke: Macmillan.

Cleaver, H, Unell, I and Aldgate, J (1999) *Children's needs – parenting capacity: the impact of parental mental illness, problem alcohol and drug use, and domestic violence on children's development.* London: The Stationery Office.

Colton, M, Drury, C, et al., (1995) *Children in need: Family support under the Children Act 1989.* Aldershot: Avebury.

Colton, M, Sanders, R and Williams, M (2001) *An introduction to working with children.* Basingstoke: Palgrave.

Corby, B (2006) *Child abuse: Towards a knowledge base, third edition.* Buckingham: Open University Press.

Crawford, K and Walker, J (2007) *Social work and human development.* Exeter: Learning Matters.

Curtis Committee (1946) Report of the Care of Children Committee Cmnd 6922. London: HMSO.

Daniel, B, Wassell, S and Gilligan, R (1999) *Child development for child care and protection workers.* London: Jessica Kingsley.

De Mause, L (1976) *The history of childhood.* London: Souvenir Press.

Department for Children Schools and Families, White Paper, *Care matters :Transforming the lives of children and young people in care*, June 2007 The Stationery Office **www.dcsf.gov.uk**.

Department for Education and Employment (2000) *Guidance on the education of children and young people in public care*. London: The Stationery Office.

Department for Education and Skills (2007) *Aiming High for Children.* London: The Stationery Office.

Department for Education and Skills (2007) *Aiming high for disabled children: Better support for families*. London: The Stationery Office.

Department for Education and Skills (2002) *Children Act Report 2002.* London: The Stationery Office.

Department for Education and Skills (2004) *Every child matters: Change for children in social care*. London: The Stationery Office.

Department for Education and Skills (2006) *Working together to safeguard children).* London: The Stationery Office.

Department of Health (1988) *Protecting children: A guide for social workers undertaking a comprehensive assessment* (the Orange Book). London: HMSO.

Department of Health (1995a) *Child protection: Messages from research*. London: HMSO.

Department of Health (1995b) *The challenge of partnership in child protection: Practice guide*. London: HMSO.

Department of Health (1996) *Reporting to court under the Children Act 1989: A handbook for social services*. London: HMSO.

Department of Health (1998a) *Disabled children: Directions for their future care*. London: The Stationery Office.

Department of Health (1998b) *Quality protects*. London: The Stationery Office.

Department of Health (1999a) *Children in the looked after system*. London: The Stationery Office.

Department of Health (1999b) *Opportunity for all: Tackling poverty and social exclusion*. London. The Stationery Office.

Department of Health (2000a) *Assessing children in need: Practice guidance*. London: The Stationery Office.

Department of Health (2000b) *Framework for the assessment of children in need and their families*. London: The Stationery Office.

Department of Health (2000c) *Lost in care (the Waterhouse Report).* London: The Stationery Office.

Department of Health (2001a) *Children looked after by local authorities, year ending 31 March 2001(A/F01/12)*. London: The Stationery Office.

Department of Health (2001b) *Children's homes' regulations*. London: The Stationery Office.

Department of Health (2001c) *National minimum care standards for children's homes*. London: The Stationery Office.

Department of Health (2001d) *The Children Act now: Messages from research*. The Stationery Office.

Department of Health (2002a) *Fostering services regulations*. London: The Stationery Office.

Department of Health (2002b) *National minimum standards for fostering services*. London: The Stationery Office.

Department of Health (2006) Safeguarding children: Guidance for Lloyd, N and Rafferty, A (2006) Black and ethnic minority families and Sure Start. Findings from Local Evaluation Reports. London. Birkbeck College.

Department of Health (2002c) *Safeguarding children in whom illness is fabricated or induced*. London: Department of Health Publications.

Department of Health (2003a) *Choice protects.* London: The Stationery Office.

Department of Health and Social Security (1974) *The report of the committee of inquiry into the care and supervision provided in relation to Maria Colwell*. London: HMSO.

Department of Health and Social Security (1988) *The report of the inquiry into child abuse in Cleveland (Butler-Sloss inquiry)*. London: HMSO.

Department of Health and the Home Office (2003) *The Victoria Climbié inquiry: Report of an inquiry by Lord Laming*. London: The Stationery Office.

Department for Work and Pensions (2004) *Family resources survey 2002–3.* **www.dwp.gov.uk**

Dobson, B and Middleton, S (1998) *Paying to care: The cost of childhood disability*. York: York Publishing Services.

Douglas, A and Philpot, T (1998) *Caring and coping*. London: Routledge.

Fahlberg, V (2004) *A child's journey through placement*. London: British Association for Adoption and Fostering.

Falkov, A (1996) *Fatal child abuse and parental psychiatric disorder*. London: Department of Health.

Featherstone, B (2004) *Family life and family support*. Basingstoke: Palgrave Macmillan.

Ferguson, H (1990) Rethinking child protection practices: A case for history, cited in the *Violence against children study group, taking child abuse seriously*. London: Unwin Hyman.

Ferguson, H (2005) *Blame culture in child protection*. Guardian, 16 January.

Flynn, R (2002) *Short breaks: Providing better access and more choice for Black disabled children and their parents*. Bristol: Policy Press.

Fox-Harding, L (1991) *Perspectives in child care policy*. Harlow: Longman.

Frost, N (2003) Understanding family support: theories, concepts and issues. In N, Frost, A Lloyd and L Jeffrey, *Companion to family support*. Lyme Regis: Russell House Publishing.

Frost, N and Stein, M (1989) *The politics of child welfare: Inequality, power and change*. Hemel Hempstead: Harvester Wheatsheaf.

Frost, N, Lloyd, A and Jeffrey, A (2003) *The RHP companion to family support*. Lyme Regis: Russell House.

General Social Care Council (2002) *Codes of practice for social care workers and employers*. London: GSCC.

Gordon, L (1989) *Heroes of their own lives: The politics and history of family violence*. London: Virago – cited in Corby (2000) op cit.

Greco, V, Sloper, P and Barton, K (2004) Care co-ordination and key worker services for disabled children in the UK. In *Research works 2004–01*. Social Policy Research Unit, University of York.

Hearn, B (1995) *Child and family support and protection: A practical approach*. London: National Children's Bureau.

Hill, N (2004) *Childcare strategy fails minority families. Guardian*, 8 December.

Holman, B (1987) Family centre. *Children and Society 2*: 157–173.

Holman, B (1988) *Putting families first. Prevention and child care*. Basingstoke. Macmillan.

Home Office (1998) *Supporting families: A consultation document*. London: The Stationery Office.

Horwath, J (ed), (2001) *The child's world: Assessing need in children*. London: Jessica Kingsley Publishers.

Human Rights Act (1998) London: The Stationery Office.

Hunt, J, Waterhouse, S and Lutman, E (2007) *Keeping them in the family: Outcomes for abused and neglected children placed with family or friends carers through care proceedings*. University of Oxford/DfES.

Ince, L (1998) *Making it alone: A study of the care experiences of young Black people*. London: British Association for Adoption and Fostering.

Iwaniec, D (1995) *The emotionally abused and neglected child: Identification, assessment and intervention*. Chichester: John Wiley.

Johns, R (2007) *Using the law in social work*. Third edition. Learning Matters

Johnson, P (1990) *Child abuse: Understanding the problem*. Marlborough: Crowood Press.

Kirton, D (2000) *Race, ethnicity and adoption*. Buckingham: Open University Press.

Koris, J (1987) *Health visitor involvement in a family centre*. Health Visitor 60: 43–44.

Lenehan, C (2004) *Speech at Early Support Programme launch*: Manchester.

Levy, A and Kahan, B (1991) *The pindown experience and the protection of children: The report of the Staffordshire Child Care Enquiry 1990*. Stafford: Staffordshire County Council.

Lindon, J (2003) *Child protection* 2nd edition. Bristol: Hodder Arnold.

Lloyd, N and Rafferty, A (2006) *Black and ethnic minority families and Sure Start findings from Local Education Reports*. London: Birkbeck Cllege.

London Borough of Brent (1985) *A child in trust. The report of the Panel of Inquiry into the circumstances surrounding the death of Jasmine Beckford.*

Lord, J, and Cullen, D (2006) *Effective panels: Guidance on regulations, process and good practice in adoption and permanence panels*. London: British Association for Adoption and Fostering.

Lowe, N and Murch, M (1999) *The plan for the child: Adoption or long-term fostering*. London: British Association for Adoption and Fostering.

Makins, V (1997) *Not just a nursery … multi-agency early years centres in action*. London: National Children's Bureau.

Marchant, R (2001) Working with disabled children. In Foley, et al., (eds) *Children in society: Contemporary theory, policy and practice*. Palgrave: Basingstoke.

Marchant, R and Gordon, R (2001) *Two-way street*. York: Joseph Rowntree Foundation.

Marks, D (1999a) Dimensions of oppression: Theorising the embodied subject. *Disability and Society*, Vol.14, No.5 pp611–26.

Marsh, P and Crow, G (1997) *Family group conferences in child welfare*. Oxford: Blackwells.

Middleton, L (1996) *Making a difference: Social work with disabled children*. Birmingham: Venture Press.

Millam, R (2002) *Anti-discriminatory practice*. London: Continuum.

Morris, J (1995) *Gone missing? A research and policy review of disabled children living away from their families*. London: Who Cares? Trust.

Morris, J (1998a) *Still missing? Vol.2 Disabled children and the Children Act*. London: Who Cares? Trust.

Morris, J (1998b) *Don't leave us out: Involving children and young people with communication impairments*. York: York Publishing Services.

Morris, J (1999) *Hurtling into the void: Transition to adulthood for young people with 'complex health and support needs'*. Brighton: JRF Pavilion.

Munro, E (1999) Common errors in reasoning in child protection. *Journal of Child Abuse and Neglect*, Volume 23, 8, pp745–758.

Murphy, M (2004) *Developing collaborative relationships in interagency child protection work*. Lyme Regis: Russell House Publications.

National Audit Office (2006) *Sure Start children's centres*. London. The Stationery Office.

O'Brien, J (2002) *Person centred planning*. Toronto: Inclusion Press.

Oldman, C and Beresford, B (1998) *Homes unfit for children*. Basingstoke: Polity Press.

Oliver, M (1983) *Social work with disabled people*. Basingstoke: Macmillan.

Oliver, M (1990) *The politics of disablement*. Basingstoke: Macmillan.

OPCS (Office of Population and Censuses and Surveys) (1986) *Surveys of disability in Great Britain, Reports 1–6*. London: HMSO.

O' Hagan, K (2006) *Identifying emotional and psychological abuse*. Buckingham: Open University Press.

Parker, R (ed) (1999) *Adoption now: Messages from research*. London: Department of Health.

Parrot, L (2007) *Values and ethics in social work practice*. Exeter: Learning Matters.

Parton, N (2001) Protecting children: A Socio-Historical Analysis. In K Wilson, and A James (eds) *The child protection handbook*. London: Balliere Tindall.

Performance and Innovation Unit (2000) *Prime Minister's review of adoption*. London: The Cabinet Office.

Platts, H, Hughes, J, Lenehan, C and Morris, S (1996) *We miss her when she goes away: Respite services for children with learning disabilities and complex health needs*. Manchester: NDT.

Quinton, D (2004) *Supporting parents: Messages from research*. London: Jessica Kingsley.

Randall, P and Parker, J (1999) *Supporting the families of children with autism*. Chichester: John Wiley.

Replacement Children Act (1989) *Guidance on private fostering* (2005) London: DfES.

Report of the Home Office Advisory Group on Video Evidence (1989). London: HMSO.

Review of Children's Cases (Amendment) (England) Regulations 2004.

Rose, W (1994) *An overview of the developments of services – the relationship between protection and family support and the intentions of the Children Act 1989*. Sief Conference, September.

Rowntree, S (1901) *Poverty: A study in town life*. London: Macmillan.

Russell, P (1995) Positive choices: *Services for children with disabilities living away from home*. London: National Children's Bureau.

Scott, J and Ward, H (Eds) (2005) *Safeguarding and promoting the well-being of children, families and communities*. London: Jessica Kingsley.

Seden, J, Sinclair, R, Robbins, D and Pont, C (2001) *Studies informing the framework for the assessment of children in need and their families*. Department of Health. London: The Stationery Office.

Seebohm Report (1968) *Report of the committee on local authority and allied personal services* Cmnd 3703. London: HMSO.

Sellick, C and Howell, D (2003) *Innovative, tried and tested: A review of good practice in fostering*. London: Social Care Institute for Excellence.

Shah, R (1995) *The silent minority: Children with disabilities in Asian families*. Derby: National Children's Bureau.

Sinclair, R and Carr-Hill, R (1997) *The categorisation of children in need*. London: National Children's Bureau.

Smith, F and Brann, C with Cullen, D and Lane, M (2004) *Fostering now*. London: British Association for Adoption and Fostering.

Statutory Instrument (1991) **No. 895 Review of children's cases regulations** (1991) London: The Stationery Office.

Statutory Instrument (2004) No. 1419 Review of children's cases (2004) *(Amendment) England Regulations*. London: The Stationery Office.

Stones, C (1994) *Focus on families. Family centres in action*. Basingstoke: Macmillan.

Swain, J, Finkelstein, V, French, S and Oliver, M (eds) (1993) *Disabling barriers – enabling environments*. London: Sage

The Advocacy Services and Representations Procedure (Children) (Amendment) Regulations (2004) SI719. London: The Stationery Office.

The Stationery Office (2006) *Working together to safeguard children*.

The Children (Private Arrangements for Fostering) Regulations 2005

Topss UK Partnership (2003) *National occupational standards for managers in residential care*. Topss UK Partnership.

Tunstill, J and Aldgate, J (2000) *Services for children in need, from policy to practice*. London: The Stationery Office.

Tunstill, J, Aldgate, J and Hughes, M. (2007) *Improving children's services networks. Lessons from Family Centres*. London and Philadelphia: Jessica Kingsley.

Tunstill, J, Allnock, D, et al., (2002) *Sure Start national evaluation*. Nottingham: Department for Education and Skills.

Tunstill, J, Hughes, M, et al., (2004) Family support at the centre: Family centres, services and networks. In D Quinton *Supporting parents: Messages from research*, London: Jessica Kingsley.

Unsworth, L (2004) *Choice, power, performance: The need for information on care services in England*. London: The Stationery Office.

Utting, W (1991) *Children in the public care: A review of residential child care*. London: HMSO.

Warner, N (1992) *Choosing with care*. London: HMSO.

Warren, C (1998) *Family centres and their role in community development. Family Support Network Newsletter* (13): 14–20.

Waterhouse, S (1997) *The organisation of fostering services*. London: NFCA.

Watson, N, Shakespeare, T, Cunningham-Burley, S and Barnes, C (1999) *Life as a disabled child: A qualitative study of young people's experiences and perspectives. Final report of an ESRC-funded study*. Edinburgh: University of Edinburgh.

Westcott, H and Cross, M (1996) *This far and no further: Towards ending the abuse of disabled children*. Birmingham: Venture Press.

Whalley, M (1994) *Learning to be strong. Setting up a neighbourhood service for under 5's and their families*. London. Hodder and Stoughton.

Wilson, K, Sinclair, I, Taylor, C, Pithouse, A and Sellick, C (2004) *Fostering success: An exploration of the research literature in foster care*. London: Social Care Institute for Excellence.

Wooley, P V and Evans, W A (1955) The significance of skeletal lesion in infants resembling those of Traumatic Origin. *Journal of the American Medical Association* No 158, 7.

www.baaf.org.uk
www.ccnuk.org.uk

www.connexions.gov.uk

www.contactafamily.co.uk

www.councilfordisabledchildren.co.uk

www.dfes.org.uk

www.doh.org.uk

www.espp.org.uk

www.fostering.net

www.jrf.co.uk

www.ness.gov.uk

www.rightfromthestart.org.uk

www.sharedcarenetwork.co.uk

www.surestart.gov.uk/surestar

Index

Transforming Social Work Practice – titles in the series

To order, please contact our distributor: BEBC Distribution, Albion Close, Parkstone, Poole, BH12 3LL. Telephone: 0845 230 9000, email: **learningmatters@bebc.co.uk**. You can also find more information on each of these titles and our other learning resources at www.learningmatters.co.uk.